Waves of God's Embrace

Waves of God's Embrace:

Sacred Perspectives from the Ocean

Winston Halapua

CANTERBURY
PRESS
Norwich

© Winston Halapua 2008

First published in 2008 by the Canterbury Press Norwich
(a publishing imprint of Hymns Ancient & Modern Limited,
a registered charity)
13–17 Long Lane, London EC1A 9PN

www.scm-canterburypress.co.uk

British Library Cataloguing in Publication data

A catalogue record for this book is available
from the British Library

ISBN 978-1-85311-922-4

Typeset by Regent Typesetting, London
Printed and bound by
CPI Bookmarque, Croydon, CRO 4TD

Contents

Foreword

I look from my study down to the waters of the Waitemata Harbour – 'the sparkling waters' with the brooding volcano, Rangitoto, in the background. Winston Halapua in this book draws on his regular encounter with this place – the sea and the sight of the island volcano. With beguiling simplicity he develops the metaphor of the sea and the great oceans and draws from them images that reflect on personal identity, relationships, sharing and hospitality between people, deep encounters through story-telling, poetry reflecting under-standings of God and the place of human beings as part of creation.

The stories of a boy with a makeshift driftwood canoe anticipating the future; Winston and his father catching fish from the sea to feed their family; the story of a pectoral cross once belonging to St Peter Chanel being given to Fine Halapua when he was consecrated as an Anglican bishop and now worn by Winston; the sharing of food on the altar of the Anglican cathedral in Suva, Fiji, with people after sheltering from a hurricane; – these stories and more are parables of hope, grace, ecumenical friendship and generosity. The stories emerge from life in Oceania where the sea is not seen as boundary or limitation but as part of the created order.

The threat of global warming and its adverse impact on small low lying islands like Tuvalu is a present threat with the danger of future catastrophe for its inhabitants requiring immediate action. Winston links the present reality with the prophetic statement of the Pacific Conference of Churches on Climate Change. As an Anglican bishop, Winston also reflects on the tensions within his own Communion and offers the richness of the image of Oceania to highlight the 'great need to celebrate the richness of diversity'.

In bringing together God and Oceania Winston offers '*theomoana*' – 'God the Ocean' – as a metaphor to open up new ways of seeing and understanding the challenges that come from creation, the environment, the church and the ways we relate to one another. Seas can be powerful and destructive forces; but the Pacific Ocean that has given birth to Winston's '*theomoana*' takes its name from 'Pacific' meaning 'the peaceful sea'. The book's invitation is to ride the waves of peace and justice, and to join the dancing waves through the 'celebration of loving communion'.

Allan K. Davidson

An Invitation from Oceania

A walk by the ocean

Early in the morning most days of the week, I walk beside the ocean at Mission Bay or St Heliers Bay in the eastern part of Auckland. This walking has been part of my life for over ten years, since I arrived in New Zealand from the Pacific Islands. Different tides, the blowing of the winds, the changing of the weather mean that each morning the white sand is graced with a variety of deposits from the ocean – shells, pebbles, seaweed and driftwood. Each day of the year the shoreline is different. As I walk, I tread on layers of broken shell, shells scrunching under the weight of my footsteps. On the shoreline, as I ponder and dream or as I am absorbed by anxieties or the demands of the day or week, there is a crunching rhythm to my sand-sinking footsteps.

There is another rhythm as the waves lace the shore, receding and then moving forward and spreading on the beach again and again and again. As the waves embrace the sand, each wave is different. Wave after wave breaks with the sh . . . shish of the sea making music with the land, and the waves, one after another, speak of dynamics in the wider Pacific ocean, of waves beyond the horizon, of greater depths and other oceans and other shores.

The waves as they embrace the sands of Mission Bay and

St Heliers Bay dance in harmony with different weather patterns. There are gentle ripples, foaming large waves and the high angry waves when the air stings with spray. The sun rises in the east and the moon leaves the sky; I marvel at the gravitational pull of the moon and sun and the rotation of the earth and moon which produce the tides. I am aware of being embraced by the mystery and energy of a cosmic rhythm.

The morning breeze or wind breathes the fresh air of the new day in my face. As dawn breaks, I feel and hear and see creation. Unconsciously, with each step I make on the sand, burdens are often lightened and my mind is refreshed.

An invitation

Occasionally I am joined by Sue on my walk. My life's companion is not Polynesian. Her mariner ancestors may have sailed the South Seas on trading vessels and she shares a passion for the ocean. Throwing off shoes she walks where the waves meet the sand and often she stops to examine a pebble or shell.

This book was conceived in the early morning walks and I offer you an invitation to walk alongside my sharing of insights; to participate in the exploration set out in this writing, to find your own passion and to make your own discoveries.

Rangitoto and origin of the book

The volcanic island of Rangitoto lies across from the bays, at the entrance of the Waitemata Harbour. Rangitoto, an icon to Auckland, was formed about 600 years ago from a massive volcanic eruption. The island emerged from the depths of the ocean in a series of fierce explosions. It is thought that the eruption happened with little warning and was witnessed by Maori, the indigenous people of New Zealand, who lived nearby on Motutapu Island. The Maori named the new island Rangitoto: 'The Bloody Skies'. The striking island with its symmetrical cone stretches out peacefully, belying its origins, but it bears the name of the experience of the Maori who witnessed the blood-red skies of its birth from the ocean. Rangitoto, now part of the landscape of the city of Auckland, daily heralds something of the mystery of a birthing.

There is a sense in which this book emerges from the fires of my inner life. It is a lava flow of passion. It has emerged as I have walked beside the sea, as I have known myself as much a person of the ocean as my Polynesian ancestors. I am a Polynesian, who over the years has studied both theology and sociology – both disciplines heavily influenced by Western scholarship. I have been exposed to wide learning for which I have been most grateful.

But now I feel compelled to write from a great need to be authentic, to give heed to inner stirrings, to articulate that God is to be encountered in experience within this immense and pulsating universe. I write because I believe that concepts and values from Oceania have a wider relevance. Theology has in a sense been landlocked – I write using metaphors arising from the different aspects and waves of the ocean. I write with a deep oceanic sense of interconnectedness with creation, with others and with the mystery of the God who calls into being all things.

The ancient Polynesian word *moana*

The ancient Polynesian word *moana* means ocean. It is a word that remains in use in many parts of Oceania today. In Hawaii in the north, the word *moana* is used. It is used also in French Polynesia in the east of Oceania. It is used by

Maori in the south and in the west, in some parts of the Solomon Islands and in Papua New Guinea. Moana is a popular Oceanic woman's name.

Moana in many parts of Oceania speaks of the mystery of the depths of the sea. The *moana* flows into the coastal seas, which shape the reefs and the islands. There are other words used for the sea surrounding the land, the sea over the reef, the sea over the sand, the sea that drops from the land into deep waters, the sea that flows into mangroves, which harbour rich supplies of crab and fish, the coastal sea with big waves for surfing and the lagoon. When the appropriate indigenous word for a particular context of the coastal sea is used, Oceanic people know the environment, the habitat, the potentialities and dangers, and are enabled to equip themselves with the necessary tools, whether the decision is to explore, to fish or to enjoy the sea.

The *moana* is the ancient pathway. Oceanic people have held ancient beliefs in the continuation of life after death. The ancestral home was traditionally located in the eastern part of the ocean, the logical site in relation to the location of the rising sun. The ancient belief was that when a tribal person whose life was integrated well with the ancestral values died, his or her spirit travelled on to that eastern place of the rising sun. The *moana* is the pathway by which spirits of the dead from all directions of Oceania find their way home. Cape Reinga is at the far north of the North Island of New Zealand. Off Cape Reinga the Tasman Sea to the west and the Pacific Ocean to the east merge, creating unsettled water. Cape Reinga is a place of breathtaking beauty held sacred by Maori. The Maori word *reinga* means leap. Another name used for Cape Reinga is Te Rerenga Wairua, meaning 'Leaping-off Place of Spirits'. Maori names speak of the ancient Maori belief that from this sacred place the spirits of the dead depart from the land on the journey to the afterlife – to the spiritual homeland of Hawaiki in the east.

Oceanic people traditionally have observed the time of death and burial with many rituals to ensure the safe journey of the spirit. This tradition has been translated into Christian practice as families have gathered to offer prayers for the soul of the departed and to secure the welfare of the extended household.

For Oceanic people the ocean is not a vast empty space. The *moana* holds mystery because of the depths of the ocean and its hidden life. Here is experienced the presence of gods of the ocean and the spirits of the ancestors. Even in the perils of the ocean there is always a sense of affinity with those who have crossed the ocean before. In the midst of the *moana* there is a sense of being embraced – we are not alone. There is a strong sense of awe and of being in the presence of the heavenly bodies – the sun, the moon and the stars.

In his recent book, *Vaka Moana: Voyages of the Ancestors*, Kerry Howe provides the latest scientific information about the origins of the people of the Pacific. The Oceanic ancestors launched into the unknown and the mystery of the oceanic world: 'Between 3–4000 years ago the ancestors of today's Pacific peoples developed the world's first blue-water sailing technology – they engineered sophisticated ocean going vessels capable of ranging thousands of kilometres over oceans, and they created a reliable navigational system based on observations of the sea and sky' (p. 11). The Oceanic ancestors by their observation of the heavenly bodies, the movements and the dynamics of the ocean and the relationship to the land were led to honour the interconnectedness between the *moana*, the sky and the scattered islands. For the people Howe calls 'the first truly maritime people of the world', the *moana* provided the venue to experience the triune interconnectedness of the vast ocean, the sky and the dotted scattered islands.

At the origins of the Oceanic way of life was an exploration of the interconnectedness of key and fundamental components of the creation. It was a finding of new ways forward in constant relationship with the dynamics of the *moana*.

The Oceanic interconnectedness of the *fonua* and *moana*

In the Kingdom of Tonga, the Cook Islands, Samoa, Niue and Tuvalu, *fonua* is the word used for land. In Fiji the word is *vanua*, in French Polynesia it is *fenua* and the Maori word is *whenua*. In Oceania, although different words are used for land throughout, it can be argued that these are similar words varying only by a few letters. The Oceanic concept *whenua*, *vanua*, *fonua*, or *fenua* is a concept that expresses motherhood, womb, placenta, plantation or land in general. My *fonua* in Tonga is the family land, which will be inherited by my eldest son.

For an understanding of *fonua*, it is important to grasp the connection with the foremost cradle of human life – the womb. *Fonua* is the word for the womb as well as the word used for the land. Polynesians to this day honour the *fonua* as a womb from which new life springs. When our two sons were born, their *pito* (part of the umbilical cord) were carefully taken from Fiji to Tonga to the family *fonua*. The *pito* were buried in the *fonua*, one with a coconut tree and one with a rare flowering shrub. The burying of part of the after-birth is also a traditional way of expressing deep connections. By the traditional burying of the *pito*, we are acknowledging that our sons are rooted in the land of their forebears and the life of the people. Celine Hoiore, a New Testament Scholar from French Polynesia, writes, 'When the pito (umbilical cord) drops off, the father of the child buries it inside the family land where he or she is born, marked either by a stone, flower or tree or it is thrown into the sea. This tradition symbolised the fact that an individual is born or rooted in a specific place. This ritual is still practised today' (2003, p. 58). She goes on to explain: 'This ritual of burying the *pu fenua* [placenta] and the *pito* is to guarantee and to affirm the close relationship between an individual and his/her land. It is a symbol of their unity and integration. For, as the infant was attached and nourished through the *pito* in his/her mother's womb, so also the child is attached to the land and all life from it.' It is the Oceanic understanding that we do not own the ocean or the sea, we are owned by them.

The Fijian word for land is *vanua*. '*Vanua* does not only link the ancestors to the present situation but offers a way of life with a sense of belonging and security in the future. This sense of a strong bond that connects people with deep emotional links to one another and to the environment, the sea, mountains, rivers, land, sky and all creatures exists as common denominator in the explanations of the *vanua* presented by Fijians of different orientations' (Halapua, 2003, p. 83).

The two words *fonua* and *moana* have an intertwined and integrated rhythm in Oceania. For Oceanic people both land and ocean are the habitat of human beings and all other forms of life. *Fonua* and *moana* belong together because experience of the land and the ocean cannot be separated. People in different parts of the world who have lived with less of the ocean–land connection may have less of a sense of the mystery of the vast ocean and its relation to humanity.

The purpose of this book

We live in a world where there is an overwhelming need to learn to relate to each other and the world around us. Our failure in relationships contributes to poverty in many forms, but there are more than enough resources in this world to go round and be shared. The violence in our world both to people and to the environment, causing climate change, calls urgently for a prophetic pathway out of the doom of our own creation. We live in a world of many peoples and many challenges and opportunities. Globalization and technology may be promoting some forms of communication, but ease of communication does not necessarily lead to good and creative relationships. Groaning and glaring poverty is not so much the result of lack of resources as of our isolation from one another – our failure to realize the depth of our connection.

This book provides a perspective from Oceania. It uses Oceanic language and developed metaphor which, I would argue, have the potential to speak to the depth of our common humanity. The context of unrest and the breakdown of life-giving relationships shape the purpose of this book, which aims to point to a way forward for the emergence of creative and imaginative relationships both in the Church and in the wider world of many peoples on this amazing planet.

The contribution of Epeli Hau'ofa with his understanding of Oceania

Epeli Hau'ofa, a Pacific anthropologist, puts forward a redefinition of the Oceanic identity. This new understanding empowers some leading theologians in Oceania, including myself. Hau'ofa contends that for many years the groups of Pacific Islands have been seen in the context of isolation, smallness, underdevelopment and dependency. In his contribution to the book, *A New Oceania: Rediscovering our Sea of Islands*, he suggests that it is important that we reframe our thinking about the Pacific Islands. If we perpetuate prevalent thinking and see Pacific people as identified with small pieces of land and fail to see their wider context – the context of the immense ocean, which links the island groups and gives life to the people – then we will maintain a mentality of smallness. Hau'ofa's vision attempts to free island people from an imposed world view that maintains dependency, inferiority and helplessness. People cannot be free to develop themselves to their maximum potential if they are defined by the limited vision of others.

For Hau'ofa, it is important that Pacific people intentionally depart from ideological constraints. He argues that holding on to the name 'Pacific' perpetuates and maintains that mentality of smallness. The name 'Pacific' was imposed from another part of the world at a particular period of time by people who did not fully recognize the huge importance of the ocean as a context for the islands. Hau'ofa argues that the islands are connected by the ocean. The emphasis is placed on the ocean and its inclusiveness, embracing all the islands.

Hau'ofa contributes to helping the people of Oceania give voice to celebrating an identity that is not defined by outside perceptions. He encourages them to recognize the huge significance of the ocean as their environment and source of life. Hau'ofa, contemporary scholar and colleague, has provided inspiration for me to reflect deeply through my Oceanic heritage in engaging with both global and local issues.

Some strengths of *moana* as metaphor

The word metaphor is based on two Greek words that together mean 'to carry over', and so metaphors provide picture language that enables us to carry over meaning from one context to another. They are tools of the human imagination to help us see more clearly and to provide insights into reality. *Moana* in the Oceanic world refers to the ocean, which resonates with mystery and deep connection with human life. *Moana* with its width and depths and power provides a rich metaphor that enables us to reclaim relationships as a gift of creation to be nourished and celebrated.

The moana – all the oceans and the seas

Our planet is called *The Blue Planet* in the title of a book on the natural history of the oceans by Andrew Byatt, Alastair Fothergill and Martha Holmes. From outer space the predominant colour of the earth is blue. As much as 70 per cent of the surface of the earth is water. The five oceans of the world are the Pacific Ocean, the Atlantic Ocean, the Indian Ocean, the Arctic Ocean and the Antarctic or Southern Ocean. Oceans from different parts of world flow into each other. *Moana* is a word that embraces all oceans in unity with all creation.

From time immemorial Oceanic people have understood the life of the *moana* as an experience of oneness. The activities of the *moana* are always in relationship – the currents, the rhythm of the waves, both in the depths and on the surface, interacting with heavenly bodies and the land. The *moana* with its awesome aspects, serenity, perils and turbulence cannot be *moana* without the other oceans and seas. The *moana* as ocean flowing into the lagoon of a small island is one with a life-giving interconnected world. As a metaphor, *moana* speaks of interconnectedness.

The link with land and sky and humanity

Human beings have always been on the move. Khalid Koser states in his book, *International Migration*, that 'The history of migration begins with the origins of mankind in the Rift Valley in Africa, from where between about 1.5 million and

500 BC *homo erectus* and *homo sapiens* spread initially into Europe and later into other continents' (p. 1). Mass migrations brought people to South East Asia, and many scholars suggest that these people were the ancestors of the Oceanic people – the people today called Polynesians, Micronesians and Melanesians (Patrick Vinton Kirch, 1997).[1] From South East Asia human beings ended a journey on foot and over land. As they reached the uncharted ocean, new ways forward were to be found. By painstaking observation of the behaviour and the mystery of the ocean, the heavens, the winds, the impact of the land, the ancestors were able to learn the skills of navigation and to build the *vaka* – outrigger canoes – to meet the deep human yearning for exploration. The original *moana* people found the courage to meet the challenge of penetrating the mystery of the great expanses and depths of Oceania. Reflecting on their multidimensional experience on and within the waves, pioneering ancestors found keys to unlock secrets of *moana* life and were able to move towards new horizons. A distinct contribution of the pioneering *moana* people to the whole movement of humanity over the ages is their knowledge of the ocean and the wisdom that sprang from their engagement with the experience of an interconnected source of life – the *moana*.

Moana as a metaphor holds the good news that all creation is interconnected. Each component in the atmosphere, in the ocean, on the land, finds its origin, definition, purpose, completion and continuity in relationship. Life in relationship is the essence of the *moana* and all its rhythm.

---

1 Polynesia, Micronesia and Melanesia. The name Polynesia is derived from two Greek words *poly* (many) and *nesos* (island). Melanesia uses the Greek word *melos* (black) and Micronesia *micros* (small) (Brij V. Lal and Kate Fortune, 2000, p. 63). The naming of the different regions of the Pacific Ocean was by people from Europe.

Waves

To observe the ocean is to contemplate movement, even on a still day when the waves are more like the heaving of water or when the calm is so great there are only ripples, perhaps from a diving sea bird breaking the surface or a fish emerging from beneath. The ocean is like a living being. To experience the ocean is to experience immense energy, as those who plunge into the breakers or ride on the surf of incoming waves or sail buffeted by a storm know well. 'Waves are disturbances in the ocean that transmit energy from one place to another. The most familiar types of waves – the ones that cause boats to bob up and down on the open sea and dissipate as breakers on beaches – are generated by wind on the ocean surface' (Cousteau, 2006, p. 76). The tides are waves that are the result of the gravitational pull of the moon and the sun.

Waves have appealed to the human imagination as far back as history can recount. It is recorded that: 'Aristotle (384–322 BC) observed the existence of a relationship between wind and waves, and the nature of this relationship has been a subject ever since' (*Waves, Tides and Shallow Water Processes*, 1989, p. 11). Oceanic people have gone beyond observance. The characteristics, the behaviour, the wrath, the unpredictability and the serenity of the waves have become the rhythm of life of Oceanic people.

Waves express the rhythm of the *moana*. They faithfully embrace all islands, flat or volcanic, rugged or fringed by sandy bays. Waves embrace the diversity and differences of sizes and contours. In the eyes of the Oceanic people the waves are linked with other waves. The waves, which dance to the generous rhythm of the *moana*, dance in company with waves beyond the horizon. Waves speak of moving together (Polynesian Dance; see Chapter 4 below).

The waves of the *moana* are moving energy and waves

indiscriminately embrace. The waves are connected and they are at the meeting point of land and sea. Moving energy, embracing, connecting, meeting – these are aspects of the waves that help to contribute to the strength of *moana* as metaphor.

Waves follow one after the other. Unceasing, relentless, embracing, they give and give and give. Energy that is the result of constant interaction with the wind and the heavens is released freely. As metaphor, the waves of the *moana* speak of immense generosity and reciprocity.

Space

The *moana* provides space – space for life in all its forms, space for diversity, space for silence. In Oceania, *moana* as a metaphor speaks of space when issues are taken to a deeper level. *Moana* as space is an enormous gift to be honoured.

Moana – a pathway for exploration and discovery

The first Oceanic ancestors set out on journeys across what is now known as the Pacific Ocean. In doing so they explored and discovered what the ocean, the *moana*, held for them – new ways of relating, new knowledge of the heavens, the life of the waves and new lands. They encountered new challenges, met new adventures, became deeply aware of the wonder and mystery of creation and the power that energizes creation. Through journeys of the missionaries from Europe in the nineteenth century and through the journeys of many unsung Pacific Island missionaries, descendants of the first Polynesians and others in Oceania came to know the immense love of God revealed in Jesus Christ.

This book celebrates the first courageous journeys of the Oceanic people and traces how those journeys shaped their lives. It celebrates how the good news of Jesus Christ has been spread throughout Oceania and the belief that there are Oceanic insights and perspectives to share with the wider Church to contribute to the well-being of people beyond the shores of the Pacific. This book recognizes the journeys of the ancestors – both the first Polynesians and our ancestors in the Christian faith. By the use of the metaphor *moana*, it seeks a way to further the journey as people of faith in the twenty-first century.

Moana provides a way by which new life could be achieved for a community. *Moana* provides a large and dynamic metaphor that encourages us not towards static thinking but rather towards the flow of ideas and the embrace of differences. *Moana* as metaphor provides a pathway for exploration and discovery for us as members of the human family. By sheer breadth and depth of meaning, the *moana* has the potential to allow us to understand more fully our interconnectedness and to view justice issues in a larger context and in a new light.

The oceans are part of God's amazing creation. As such, they reveal the Creator God from whom all life continues to spring – the God of endless creative and loving activity. The oceans, gifted by God and gifting, speak of immense generosity. As the oceans catch the light of the sun, so we may find the glory of God reflected in ripples along the shore and in the tumbling of ocean breakers. We may find also that the use of the lens of the *moana* provides us with bright glimpses into God's purposes and new horizons for creation and for humanity. The *moana* is God's creation and there are sacred perspectives to be gained from contemplating its immense diversity and its depths.

2

Creative Imagination, Expanding Our Horizons and Moving Forward

O Jesus,
be the canoe
that holds me in the sea of life,
be the steer that keeps me straight,
be the outrigger that supports me in times of great
    temptation.

Let your Spirit be my sail that carries me through each day,
as I journey steadfastly
on the long voyage of life.
Amen.

Prayer of a young person from Vanuatu

Launching into the deep – the child and a piece of driftwood

As a family we have always lived close to the Pacific Ocean and when our children were small we lived in Suva, Fiji. Our elder son, when about five, was playing on a strip of sand near the University of the South Pacific. The sand was full of driftwood. He managed to find a large piece of wood and launched it into the shallows. He quickly found a small stick and sat astride the large log, using his stick as a paddle. A game, yes, but more than a game. My wife caught the expression of intent on his face – his serious eyes scanning the ocean and then fixed on the horizon. Our son's imagination was at work and he was clearly paddling across the ocean on a canoe that cleaved the waves and sped him forward to discover new lands. He was one with his ancestors who had travelled in the great *vaka* (Oceanic outrigger). As we look back, the child was anticipating his future as a young engineer with a passion for the ocean and outrigger canoeing as a serious sport.

Creative imagination and passionate concern

The story about my son and his 'canoe' is a very small story about the stirrings of the imagination but it is powerful in its profound simplicity. The ocean had captured the child's thinking and action and had enabled a journey – a moving forward of the heart and mind. The child was in touch with his genetic heritage, with his inner self and with what he might become.

This book calls us to creative imagination and proposes deep reflection on the reality of the oceans of this world. *Moana* – ocean as metaphor – will suggest alternative and courageous ways forward to address the challenges of contemporary living. Creative imagination with a decisive direction enables us to dream and become and move forward.

The reality of the oceans of the world

The ancient Oceanic people knew only one *moana* – one ocean. They navigated the vast *moana*, the ocean we now know as the Pacific Ocean. Since the emergence of the Oceanic people, the *moana* had been a huge reality in their lives. Their daily experience of the waves shaped their world view, as surely as erosion caused by the constancy of the waves provided the beaches on Pacific Island shores. Their belief system was the legacy they left to those who were to come after.

The ancient Oceanic people knew something of the vastness of the *moana* as home, highway and source of life. Scientists today have contributed to our contemporary understanding of the immensity of *moana*, which is home for a multitude of living species, including whales and plankton. Over 90 per cent of marine life lives in the waters that get sunlight. Deeper still, below the epipelagic zone, sunlight does not penetrate. Scientists are still at work discovering the creatures that exist in the darkest depths.

The whole division of the *moana* by geographers into different but interconnected oceans was unknown to ancient Oceanic people. The naming of the Pacific Ocean, the Atlantic Ocean, the Indian Ocean and the Arctic Ocean was a later event in history. At the beginning of the twenty-first century the Antarctic Ocean or Southern Ocean was recognized by the Monaco-based International Hydrographic Organization. The United States of America still has some difficulty with this addition and the naming of this ocean remains in dispute. The five oceans and the seas constitute over 70 per cent of our world surface. It is not surprising that this earth has been called 'the blue planet'.

Each ocean has a distinct geography. Each ocean has particular wonders and resources. But the named oceans are not separated or static. There is movement and there is interaction. There is diversity in the five oceans and the diversity is free flowing – the oceans flow into one another. There is dynamic interconnectedness through the strength of life-giving currents and other deep ocean currents.

The Pacific Ocean

The Pacific Ocean is the largest of all oceans and the deepest. It constitutes half of the water on the surface of this earth. It is twice the size of the Atlantic Ocean. Ferdinand Magellan (1480–1520), the Portuguese explorer, gave to this ocean the name *Mare Pacificum* (in English pacific or peaceful sea) but there are other, less peaceful realities. The Pacific Ocean is also known for its devastating hurricanes, typhoons and tsunami. Much of the Pacific rim is characterized by narrow continental shelves, which have active volcanoes and are vulnerable to earthquakes. Hawaii is a group of volcanic islands in the north-eastern part of Oceania and is well known as a destination for tourists. One of the islands, Mauna Kea, is the highest mountain in the world. When measured from the base below sea level to the peak, Mauna Kea is higher than Everest in the Himalayan ranges. The deepest trench, known as the Marianas Trench, is in the Pacific Ocean near to the Philippines. Sunlight does not penetrate into the depths of this trench. Seas in the Pacific Ocean include the Solomon Sea, Coral Sea, Arafura Sea, Banda Sea, Java Sea, Celebes Sea, Yellow Sea, Sea of Japan, Bali Sea, Bering Sea, Bering Strait, Philippine Sea, Savu Sea, Sea of Okhotsk, East and South China Seas and Tasman Sea, each of which is scattered with numerous islands (Hutchinson and Hawkins, 2004, p. 32).

One of the characteristics of the vast Pacific Ocean is the presence, in the midst of its vastness, of many tiny islands. The scattered islands are extremely isolated and remote. Many of the islands are low-lying coral islands or atolls – islands formed by coral polyps, tiny animals that use minerals from the ocean to produce protective outer skeletons. Kiritimati or Christmas Island is the world's largest coral atoll.

Clear warm seas and sunshine on shallow water are necessary for the development of coral reefs. Coral reefs are a feature of the Pacific Ocean. Reefs are an extremely ancient phenomenon, appearing around 400 million years ago. Modern forms of reef are relatively young and were formed during the last 5,000 years. Coral reefs are a home for a multitude of marine species.

The Atlantic Ocean

The Atlantic is the second largest ocean and contains important seas. It covers approximately 20 per cent of the earth's surface. The Atlantic, in comparison with the Pacific Ocean, is relatively young, having been formed around 150 million years ago. The Atlantic Ocean is not as large as the Pacific, but because the surrounding continental land masses tend to slope towards it, many of the world's great rivers drain into it.

Rivers and floods from the diverse mountainous and flat terrain carry nutrients to the shallow surface of the ocean. The wide continental shelf stretches along the shoreline of the nations surrounding the Atlantic. These waters provide nourishment for abundant marine creatures great and small. Some migrate from other oceans in search of food. The wide continental shelf, which characterizes the margins of the Atlantic Ocean, provides important commercial fishing grounds besides rich oil and gas reserves and other mineral resources exploited by industrial nations.

Included in the Atlantic Ocean are the North Sea, Irish Sea, Celtic Sea, Baltic Sea, Black Sea, Caribbean Sea, Scotia Sea, Sargasso Sea, Denmark Strait, Gulf of Mexico, Mediterranean Sea and Norwegian Sea. Featuring strongly in the oceanic activities of the Atlantic is the clockwise flowing of the currents from North America all the way to north Europe. The Atlantic Ocean is also known for its strong winds. (Based on Hutchinson and Hawkins, 2004, p. 28.)

The Indian Ocean

The Indian Ocean is bounded by the continents of Asia, Africa and Oceania. It stretches from India in the north to the Antarctic Ocean in the south and from the eastern side of the continent of Africa to the western part of Australia, and embraces the Malay Peninsula and the Sunda Islands. The Indian Ocean includes the Red Sea, Arabian Sea, Persian Gulf, Bay of Bengal, Strait of Malacca, Andaman Sea, Java Trench and Timor Sea. In recent history, the Indian Ocean experienced the world's most powerful earthquake for 40 years. This precipitated devastating tsunami.

Within the Indian Ocean, there are five major currents. Current circulation in the north-east flows in one direction, then reverses direction, twice a year. This is due to the monsoon winds. This reversing of direction is unique in comparison with other oceans. The southern Indian Ocean is dominated by an anticlockwise current.

Oil and gas are exploited in the continental shelf of the Persian Gulf and Western Australia. Most fishing resources in this ocean are in the coastal area of Asia. Fishing is predominantly for the consumption of the small communities that are scattered along the coastal regions. The limited continental shelves restrict opportunities for commercial fishing. (Based on Hutchinson and Hawkins, 2004, pp. 30–31.)

The Arctic Ocean

The North Pole provides the central point of the Arctic Ocean. The oceanic life of this region is influenced by the climate of the North Pole, which is a sea of ice, frozen all year round and varying in thickness from winter to summer. It is the smallest named ocean. It is also the shallowest. Most of the influx of fresh water is from the Siberian rivers. As the polar ice is sustained in the form of ice sheets, this region is unique and different from any of the other oceans.

Because part of the Arctic Ocean is frozen throughout the year, there is barren land in surrounding nations, which include Russia, Greenland, Iceland, Canada and Alaska. The position of the North Pole in relation to the sun results in long hours of sunshine for six months in summer. In winter the Arctic knows long hours of darkness. During summer, some of the animals and birds that have adopted the Arctic Ocean as home migrate. This region is home for the polar bear, the ringed seal and the bowhead, the Arctic whale. Contributing to the richness of this ocean are the Beaufort Sea, Barents Sea and Greenland Sea.

The Antarctic Ocean (or Southern Ocean)

In the southernmost part of the globe is the Antarctic or Southern Ocean. These are the names now given to the southern extension of the Pacific, Atlantic and Indian Oceans. This ocean is the coldest and most remote from the rest of the world. There is no rainfall (Twist, 2005, p. 38). At the same time, ice covering this ocean constitutes 70 per cent of the world's fresh water. As in the Arctic region, the severe cold climate does not attract a diversity of living species. The Antarctic Circumpolar Current flows in a clockwise direction around Antarctica and isolates the surface waters of the Antarctic Ocean from oceans to the north. The Weddell Sea, the Ross Sea, Amundsen Sea, Dumont d'Urville Sea, Davis Sea and Haakon VII Sea are all part of this ocean (based on Trewby, 2002, pp. 8–9).

The Antarctic Ocean experiences strong gusty winds and high seas during winter. In her book, *Illustrated History of Antarctica*, Marcia Stenson writes: 'Antarctic means "opposite to Arctic". It is a continent surrounded by ocean. The great plateau is the most desolate, storm-driven place on earth, much colder than the Arctic'. She continues: 'Penguins are only found in Antarctica' (p. 6). Underneath the surface of the ice is an abundant natural harvest. Currents and waves distribute phytoplankton widely to fish and other sea creatures. Antarctica is the home of creatures such as blue whales, sharks, squid, seals and penguins (see Twist, 2005, p. 35). This polar region is an ecologically important environment and is home for species that live nowhere else.

The wealth of interconnected diversity

When the five oceans are considered together, there is opportunity to celebrate the diversity they represent and the way that diversity is not locked into each ocean. Each ocean shares its diversity with other oceans. They complement each other and together they give life to planet earth. Even the oceans in the polar regions have a valuable role.

The Pacific Ocean, with both its serenity and its unpredictability, with its coral reefs, volcanic eruptions, ocean depths, vast tracts, scattered islands and immense volume of water, is hugely significant, but it does not take dominating precedence. It is the largest ocean and yet it complements the other oceans, which also have a vital role to play in the life of the planet. The very life of the Pacific Ocean needs the contribution of other oceans.

In contrast to the Pacific Ocean, the Arctic Ocean is the smallest ocean. It is partly frozen throughout the year and knows long hours of darkness in the winter months. The Pacific Ocean, with its vast amounts of warm water from the impact of sunlight in equatorial and tropical areas, needs the contribution of the Arctic Ocean. The interaction of the warm waters of the Pacific Ocean with the waters of the cold oceans contributes to the balance of oceanic temperature and life for the creatures of the oceans and the creatures of the land through its influence on climate. The warmer oceans need the colder oceans and vice versa, and the planet needs the contribution of the oceans held together and interacting. No single ocean, however large or however small, exists by itself or for itself.

The Atlantic Ocean is a significant ocean, with its wider continental shelf, the mighty rivers that drain into it, its fishing grounds and mineral and oil resources. Like the Pacific Ocean, it spans the equator and can be divided into the North Atlantic and the South Atlantic Oceans. It reaches from the Arctic Ocean to the Antarctic Ocean and its waves also meet those of the South Pacific Ocean. The resources of the Atlantic Ocean are huge. The abundance of nutrients brought down from the rivers to the wide continental shelf attracts marine life from other oceans coming in search of food.

The Indian Ocean also has unique features with its circular currents. This is the warmest ocean and provides major sea routes. The peculiar pattern of currents in the Indian Ocean may give the impression that the ocean is locked into its own particular dynamic, but in the southern hemisphere the Indian Ocean is interconnected with three others oceans – the Pacific Ocean, the Antarctic Ocean and the Atlantic Ocean.

One of the major features of the Antarctic Ocean is that it is inhospitable to most forms of life. This is because of its severe climate and the circumpolar current, the longest of all currents, which creates strong, angry seas. Even with such bleak isolation, the Antarctic still provides a home for some forms of life that live nowhere else. Within the boundaries of this ocean, the harshness of the elements produces amazing strategies of survival in the creatures that make the Antarctic their home. For the birds and whales that migrate from this region, there is an anticipation of a feast in other climes. The

Antarctic Ocean in its landless northern boundary merges into the Atlantic, Pacific and Indian Oceans.

Marcia Stenson highlights the importance of Antarctica to the world. She asserts: 'Antarctica is important to everyone in the world. Antarctica drives our weather, influencing both heat and sea levels. The thick ice cap of the high Polar Plateau and the glaciers reflect back eighty percent of the sun's heat, moderating the world's climate. Seventy per cent of the world's fresh water is locked up there. Algae from the melting glaciers feed krill, the basis of an important food chain' (p. 6).

The combined impact of the oceans – the transformation of the barrenness of the earth

Each of the oceans has distinct and fascinating features and yet wonderfully and importantly there is interconnectedness between the diverse dynamics and life of the oceans. The diversity of each ocean combines to enable the flow of life-giving energy within planet earth. Each ocean has its own distinct dynamics and features, not in isolation or competition, but in flowing waves and currents in partnership with other oceans. The waves and the currents are instrumental in distributing the various gifts of the five diverse oceans within each of them and beyond ocean boundaries. They also enable the interaction with the sun, the atmosphere and the land.

The oceans are alive with constant motion. Currents and waves flow constantly and faithfully, moving in many directions. Some currents flow clockwise and others anticlockwise. There are currents that flow on the surface. There are currents that flow in the depth of the ocean. The *moana* is powerfully alive with energy and movement. Because of this constant energy and movement, the contribution of the oceans to planet earth is widely distributed.

The oceans together provide – gift – planet earth with half of the oxygen needed for survival and help balance many atmospheric gases. Without the oceans the land would be barren. The oceans 'power the winds, feed the clouds with moisture and nourish the land; water drawn up into the atmosphere, that falls again as rain is key to keeping our planet alive. They help regulate the temperatures through the powerful currents that move warm and cold waters north and south' (Holden, 2007, p. 42).

The oceans as home

The sun is welcome on the waters of the ocean. Together the sun and the oceans produce the climate of the earth. The wind moves on the water contributing to the dance of the waves. The ocean has room, abundant room, for many species of plant and animal life. The great whales and the tiniest forms of life in the ocean have space to move, shelter, feast and carry out many other activities. Gallagher, who is the Editorial Director of the book, *1000 Facts on Oceans*, states that: 'Oceans are home to nearly 300,000 different living species, ranging from huge whales to tiny fish' (see Twist, 2005, p. 4).

Expanding our horizons

I have sketched the complementary diversity of the oceans with their flowing interconnectedness, and noted the huge impact the combined oceans have on the planet earth and that the vastness of the oceans provides both space and home for many forms of life. I invite you, the reader, to engage with your own experiences of the awe-inspiring waves.

Tiny tropical fish are often caught in pools in the coral reef when the tide recedes. The tiny fish may be forgiven for thinking that the extent of their tiny pool is the whole ocean, not just an infinitesimally small corner. They may have no imagination, but maybe even within their shining scales they have an inkling that there is an ocean far greater and wider.

But we, as human beings, do have imagination. We need not be locked into closed systems. We can move out of our parochial smallness, as I am now moving to explore a little further the *moana* as life-giving metaphor. In this chapter I am putting forward the thesis that the *moana* can awaken us to a wider acceptance and celebration of diversity. The *moana* has abundant room for diversity and that diversity is freely flowing. As we consider the oceans of the world, we may be drawn to conclude that differences may have their place and indeed contribute to the greater well-being of the whole.

Galilee – launching place of mission

The Sea of Galilee is not an actual sea but a lake. The Hebrew Bible calls the lake Chinnereth, which may refer to its harp shape. Geographically, Galilee is a lake, but in the Gospels it is referred to as the Sea of Galilee. This reference in the Gospels to sea rather than lake is interesting. In an article on 'Jesus' Galilee', Janine Kemp writes: 'With the ancient understanding of the cosmology, with the heaven above and the underworld below, the sea became a potentially hostile place where the barrier between humanity and the chaotic underworld was quite literally fluid. Thus, fishing in the first century must have been considered a risky business, and even travel by boat was at the mercy of the spiritual realm. The stories, then, of the miraculous catch of fish, the stilling of the storm, and walking on water show Jesus' divinity and power, not just over nature, but over spiritual forces, and as the "Son of God", he was Lord over the sea' (p. 9). The emphasis on sea may be a particular theological tool used in the Gospels to underline the extent to which Jesus triumphs over creation, including spiritual forces.

Jesus in Galilee transforms what is hostile into something that is life-giving. The sea is no longer a threat. The diversity of the social life on the shores of Galilee is not a threat but a means through which the early ministry of Jesus could take shape and a life-giving mission could emerge. Capernaum, the fishing town on the shores of Galilee, predominantly Jewish in population, was the base for Jesus and the first disciples. It was a base for boundary breaking. Jesus deliberately crossed the sea often and crossed boundaries going into Gentile territory.

A most unlikely place, a new place, in and across the Sea of Galilee, was the launching place of a new transforming movement. Jesus, having shaped his disciples in the diversity afforded by Galilee, was ready to move forward to the centre of religious, socio-economic and political power in Jerusalem. The mission then did not remain in Jerusalem but crossed many boundaries to the rest of the world. Jesus fired imaginations and was continually challenging his disciples to expand their horizons. The gospel of God's love was infinitely more embracing of diversity than was ever imagined. We too are called to expand our horizons.

3

The Ocean as Gifting Life

Our Pacific islands are yours, O Lord,
And all the seas that surround them.
You made the palm trees grow,
And the birds fly in the air.

When we see your beautiful rising sun
And hear the waves splash on our shores,
When we see the new moon rise
And the old moon sink,

We know, O Lord, how wonderful you are.
You bless our people;
From Truk to Tonga and beyond
You spread your caring wings.

Even when we sail through stormy seas,
And fly amidst rain clouds,
We know you await us,
With kaikai[1] and coconut.

You who turn storms into gentle winds,
And troubled seas into tranquil waters,

---

1 Kaikai: pidgin word for 'food'.

You who make yams grow
And bananas blossom,

Wash our people with justice;
Teach us with righteousness;
Speak to us daily;
Strengthen us to serve you.

A Psalm from the Pacific by Bernard Narakobi,
Papua New Guinea in *Your Will be Done*

Ancestral roots, childhood and the gifts from the ocean

Niua Toputapu, part of the Kingdom of Tonga, is a tiny remote island surrounded by the Pacific Ocean. Niua is far from Tongatapu, the main island where the capital of Tonga, Nuku'alofa, is situated. Our forebears on my paternal side are from Niua. My mother was from Mu'a, the original capital of Tonga, on the eastern coast of Tongatapu, the main island of the Kingdom. From both sides of the family, our heritage is an existence surrounded by the life-giving waves of the Pacific Ocean.

Fine, my father, was brought as a young child from remote Niua Toputapu to stay with extended family and attend the Anglican school that had just been established in the present capital, Nuku'alofa. He stayed in Nuku'alofa, becoming the first Tongan Headmaster of St Andrew's School, the first Tongan Anglican priest and eventually Bishop. As children we were brought up in Nuku'alofa near to the ocean.

Nuku'alofa means in Tongan 'The Place of Love'. There were ten children in the family and there were also cousins living with us who had come from the scattered islands and the interior. We knew love, but there was also real hardship. My parents found it very difficult to feed the family on a very minimal missionary church stipend. Meat was very scarce and unaffordable. There was little money for supplies at the store. To help the family survive, my father worked on our small plantation growing yams, bananas and other crops. Fishing was a vital activity for the feeding of our large and lively household.

At low tide, paddling in the shallows by the shore, the children collected seaweed and shellfish. My father taught during the day and at night-time he used to go fishing at low tide. I was eager to go with my father to hold the sack for the catch. The water level was below my father's knees, but well above mine. In his left hand, Fine held the benzine light to attract the fish and with his right hand he held a cane knife to intercept the dazzled fish. The timing from when the fish were spotted to when and where to hit with the knife was an art. If the catch was poor, we collected shellfish which came out at night from their sheltered places, and brought them home. What remains with me vividly is the breakfast together taking place immediately when we returned from fishing. The catch was fresh from the sea and was cooked straight away. The hungry household feasted at the break of day.

Standing in the lagoon, observing the ripples, aware of the currents and the position of the moon, my father was expert in casting a fishing net. Before school, in the early hours of the morning or after school, Dad cast his fishing net, if the weather permitted. It was both my work and a passion to accompany my father catching fish. Looking back, although we grew up in a financially struggling extended family, there was joy. We grew up healthy, fed by the abundant gifts of the ocean. Apart from catching fish and collecting shellfish and different seaweeds and even jellyfish, which we sold, hours of swimming were part of the fun and we swam like fish. The reality of my early formation taught me clearly something of the ocean and its life-giving gifts.

Oceans – the cradle of life on this planet

I began with my own story as a child on a small Pacific Island and vivid experiences of the generosity of the ocean. I now turn to an infinitely wider story – the story of the planet earth and the formation of the oceans. According to scientists, the earth's oceans formed largely from water vapour that condensed from its primitive atmosphere, and water may also have been brought to the earth by ice-laden comets.

From water vapour in the atmosphere condensing, oceans were born. 'About 4,000 million years ago, the atmosphere was dominated by water vapour, but as the earth continued cooling, water vapour in the atmosphere began to condense and fall as rain. Streams developed into rivers, and gradually low-lying areas filled with water. The oldest sedimentary (water-formed) rocks found to date suggest that these early seas formed about 38,000 million years ago' (Byatt, Fothergill and Holmes, 2001, p. 18). The Pacific Ocean is the oldest ocean on earth.

The earth is unique in our solar system because it is the only planet to have vast expanses of water. The oceans were the cradle of the earliest forms of life. Because of the water of the oceans, life on earth exists as we know it. We can say that the oceans were a primary means of gifting life on earth.

Water has transformed the earth from a hostile barren wilderness to a place where life develops and grows. The early oceans cradled life and the oceans continue to provide that which sustains and nurtures life on the planet. 'There is a constant recycling of water around the planet. As the sun heats the surfaces of oceans, water vapour rising into the atmosphere forms clouds. These are driven around the globe by winds and when the conditions are right, they condense and fall as rain, snow or hail.

The process of water changing from its liquid state in the oceans to gas in the atmosphere and back again to liquid is known as the hydrological cycle and is essential to life on land. Without it much of the world would be barren' (Byatt, Fothergill and Holmes, 2001, p. 19).

The Genesis story of creation and primordial waters

The cosmic sea is central to the biblical picture of the formation of the universe. The Israelites believed that God used a cosmic sea in the creation of the sea, the heaven and the earth. The Jewish Bible begins with the account of the creation story. The opening verse of Genesis describes God's engagement with the cosmic sea and transformation of chaos and the deep: 'In the beginning when God created the heavens and the earth, the earth was formless and void and darkness covered the face of the deep, while a wind from God swept over the face of the waters.' From waters swept by God's Spirit comes the dawn of creation; the very life of our planet is formed.

The second creation story in Genesis chapter 2 links the creation of a human being closely with water '. . . a stream would rise from the earth, and water the whole face of the ground – then the Lord God formed man from the dust of the ground and breathed into his nostrils the breath of life; and the man became a living being' (Genesis 2.6–7). And again in Genesis chapter 2 we have the wonderful picture of a well-watered fertile garden, the Garden of Eden. A river flows out of Eden, forming four branches.

An account of waters and their God-given, life-giving properties is at the beginning of the Bible. In the book of Revelation, the last book of the Bible, in the last chapter we have the vision of 'the river of the water of life, bright as crystal flowing from the throne of God and of the Lamb' (Revelation 22.1). And there is the promise to the thirsty: 'Let anyone who wishes take the water of life as a gift' (22.17).

The oceanic concept of the *manava* of life

In Chapter 1 I explained that the ocean was conceptualized by the Polynesian word *fonua*, or womb. It was seen as the source of life. If there is a source of life then there is inter-connectedness with all the created order. Contemporary scientists speak of the ecosystem. Polynesian concepts that speak of intrinsic affinity with all creation precede the concepts of modern science.

I want to develop this concept further here, using the word *manava*. *Manava* in many Pacific Islands is the word for both the womb and the placenta and it also refers to the life that is nurtured. *Manava* is life and that which nurtures life. It is a deeply spiritual word, which has to do with deep connection and relationships. When a child is born, the child is the embodiment of the *manava*. In the Oceanic world view the child never stands apart from the origins. The present and future well-being of the child are seen as connectedness to origins.

In the Hebrew Scriptures we have the idea of the breath of God, *ruach*, infusing creation with life. God breathes into the nostrils of man formed from the dust and Adam is created. In the Tongan translation, the breath of God is *manava*. And if we allow the insights of the Polynesian word *manava* to aid our reflection on creation, so we, in the gift of creation, are deeply connected to God, to other human beings and to nature in all its reality and fullness. Our well-being as people of this planet is to be found in our acknowledgement of the reality and depth of our interconnectedness with all living things and with our origins in the God of life who nurtures life.

Returning to origins

In different religious and cultural traditions, people have identified some areas of water as being sacred places. In Hinduism, a place where rivers meet is a holy place. The Ganges is a holy river and people make pilgrimages to submerge themselves in this great river. Before the advent of Christianity in England, there were places around springs of water that were regarded as sacred. To primitive people, water emerging from the earth was a great mystery and so there were holy wells. The Christian practice of making pilgrimage to certain places regarded as holy is a call to connection with a source of life. These holy places may or may not be places of springs of water, but they do have the potential to renew and refresh in the life of God's Spirit. To make pilgrimage in the present to a source of origin and life is not to remain embedded in the past but to be open to challenges ahead and to receiving and sharing new life-giving gifts.

In this book, in one sense, I am encouraging a return to origins. Reflecting on the ocean gifted by God has the creative potential to deepen our understanding of God, the source of the oceans and all life. It has the potential to make us more deeply aware just how profoundly connected we are and that as we are drenched by God's free gift of love, so we will be bearers of gifts to one another.

Polopolo – an Oceanic understanding of giving

Polopolo is an ancient Tongan word for gift. Different words for gift are used throughout Oceania. However, Oceanic people have a common understanding and world view of gifting. *Polopolo* in its essence is a gift as a portion of the whole. When Oceanic people present gifts, the nature of the gift indicates the location and the context of the giver and the position of the receiver in the community or the household. *Polopolo* is linked to the giving of the first fruits or the best portion.

The Oceanic world view of gift is deeper than the definition of 'gift' in English may imply. *Polopolo* was originally a culture of offering by people to the ancestral gods the best portion of what had already been given to them, such as the fish they had caught or the crops they had harvested. Our Oceanic forebears believed that their new home either in the interior or on the coastal land was the gift of the gods. The gods were honoured and regarded as originators. From the gods stemmed the identity of the tribe or a group of people. Giving to the gods was a returning in gratitude of something of the best, the fruits of creation. The fruits of creation were the expression of the creativity and work the gods had originated.

The resources of the location and the creativity of the people, either from the land or the sea, are expressed when gifts are offered. The best is offered. Whatever is presented bears witness to the unique gifts of the ancestors and the creativity of people today as they move to the future. The giving of gifts today in Oceania still continues to express the uniqueness of location, identity and pride when gifts of food, dance, song or artefacts are presented. *Polopolo*, in terms of giving, has to do with presenting significant free gifts that are part of a bigger legacy.

Our understanding of *polopolo* is connected to our roots and a deep appreciation, conscious or unconscious, that our life and all things around us are gifts. This understanding helps us recognize our responsibility as custodians of the legacy of the past for the sake of the future. To live shaped by the world view of *polopolo* is to live out of abundant generosity. At best, it is a response of grace for grace. It is a love offering within the abundant richness of the ancestral legacy by which people may contribute to each other what is lacking in any situation.

This chapter began with a story of living out of the abundant generosity that the Ocean provides. The call to live out of abundant generosity, to offer the best of our creativity and life, is a call today to the worldwide Church. It is a call to humanity as we live in a world where gifts of creation are abused, where nations do not always share the best of resources and where our interconnectedness as people of planet earth is not always honoured.

The abuse of the gifts of creation – Tuvalu

While the materially rich developed nations call global meetings of top scientists and politicians to discuss the issues surrounding climate change, and attempt to make decisions that will combat the huge threat that climate change poses to the future of the planet, the island state of Tuvalu is being submerged by the waves of the Pacific Ocean.

Tuvalu is one of the 16 small developing independent Pacific Island states. Tuvalu was known as the Ellice Islands before gaining its independence from Britain in 1978. To mark its independence, the people who had gained their right to determine their own destiny renamed their island home Tuvalu. The name speaks of a people with deep roots in Oceania. The name Tuvalu expresses the common kinship with their ancestors in eight regions. *Tu* refers to the authority of an ancestor, the space and place of authority. *Valu* means eight. The name of the island state speaks of a profound identity. Each region of the eight units retains its own unique ancient heritage and history of how its people migrated and settled. The standing together as eight units with distinct heritage and integrity is a model to be applauded. Tuvalu is a small group of atolls. Small can be beautiful.

Most of its people's ancestors originally came from Tonga and Samoa.

Economically, Tuvalu is like other small island states in the Pacific. Traditionally, the people of Tuvalu have gained a subsistence livelihood, and the abundant resources of the immense ocean have been part of that livelihood. Tuna has been a major component of the diet of the people. It has also been a significant export commodity. Recently, there has been a clear indication of shifting in the pattern of tuna migration. The reduction in supplies of tuna has been related to the effects of climate change with the resulting rise in sea levels.

Since contact with the West, a significant portion of the population has been used to supply cheap labour in different parts of the Pacific. Today, Tuvalu depends on Australia and New Zealand for economic survival.

Tuvalu as a nation is a member of the Pacific Islands Forum. It has voting power in the United Nations. As a regional member of the Forum, Tuvalu votes alongside nations with populations of many millions, such as India, Japan, China and the United States. Standing together in solidarity with other nations in Oceania, Tuvalu contributes a distinct voice in the world of nations.

Tuvalu, like other small Pacific nations, Niue, the Cook Islands and Tonga, has more of its people living outside it than within. Many of its people are now resident in Fiji, Niue, Australia, New Zealand and the United States. Among the benefits of this trend of migration are payments or remittances. Remittances are consistent with the Oceanic culture of kinship, especially in the context of the island states above. Remittances are the largest contributor to the economy of the nation. The sending of remittances shows how people of Tuvalu share the benefits of their labour and creativity from beyond the horizons of their ancestral home.

With limited opportunities for migration in recent years,

the present population of Tuvalu is concentrated in the capital, Funafuti. There is little paid employment. The demand for building more cement houses, to accommodate the movement of people to the urban area, is resulting in the extraction of more sand from the beach, to the detriment of the coastal areas. Coastal erosion compounded by the digging of sand from the beach has caused the invasion of sea water into land areas.

Tuvalu's hardships are compounded by the problem of climate change and the crisis of the sea level rising because of changing weather patterns caused by greenhouse gas emissions. The tragedy is a double one in that the sea level is not only rising and destroying crops, but the sea is also seeping underground. On the surface, food crops, bananas, fruit trees, medicinal plants, breadfruits and coconuts are being destroyed. Mangroves prevent coastal erosion and provide a habitat for a variety of fish and crab, but the mangrove biodiversity is endangered in Tuvalu, as in the wider Pacific.

Climate change goes hand in hand with severe flooding. Drinking water from wells has become contaminated by salt water, which has seeped into the ground water. There is flooding above and beneath. The people are now confronted with new and growing hardships, most of which are not of their own making.

If, as scientists warn, the sea level continues to rise, Tuvalu is at risk of extinction or, as expressed in the title of a paper by a Norwegian, Terje Dahl, 'Good-Bye Tuvalu'. The former Prime Minister, Kamuta Laatasi, challenged the world in one of his presentations of the story and pride of his people: 'It seems that the world does not care what happens to my people, they want to see everybody floating before they respond.' I agree with Laatasi and hope that his Oceanic wisdom will not fall on deaf ears.

This story of Tuvalu is not so much a story about a remote island state. It is rather about an Oceanic icon in which there is the potential to see ourselves. The present-day story of Tuvalu illustrates our falling short as fellow humans and our abuse of the precious gifts of creation. Tuvalu is not being destroyed as the result of tsunami caused by volcanic eruption or earthquake, but by the abuse of the gifts of creation and a failure to see that this abuse has huge consequences – the ocean is robbed of its potential to give life. We turn a blind eye to this at our peril. May the simple story of the betrayal of Tuvalu speak to those who hold powerful positions in industrial nations. May the voice of Tuvalu be heard. As human beings may we grow in our understanding that we are interconnected with the environment and that the gifts of creation are not to be abused but are to be honoured and shared.

4

The Ocean as Embrace

Some went down to the sea in ships,
doing business on the mighty waters;
they saw the deeds of the Lord,
his wondrous works in the deep.
For he commanded and raised
the stormy wind,
which lifted up the waves of the sea.
They mounted up to heaven,
they went down to the depths;
their courage melted away in their calamity;
they reeled and staggered like drunkards,
and were at their wits' end.
Then they cried to the Lord in their trouble,
and he brought them out from their distress;
he made the storm be still,
and the waves of the sea were hushed.
They were glad because they had quiet,
and he brought them to their desired haven.

Psalm 107.23–30

The oceans embrace many lands. Few nations are entirely landlocked. The embrace of the ocean may be cruel and devastating as in tsunami and rising sea levels, but the embrace of the ocean can bring life in many forms. To be embraced by the waves of the ocean presents a challenge – the challenge to move towards to the unknown.

The Hebrew Scriptures point to a God who will be with people on their journey – even their journey through the waves of the sea. The God we see in Jesus is God intimately engaged with our well-being, a God whose intention it is to bring us to our 'desired harbour', which must be one where there are safety, peace and reason for thanksgiving. This chapter sets out to encourage us on the journey of faith today. On our journey as communities of faith, we will encounter many metaphorical storms and indeed hurricanes threatening our security and well-being. The challenges of our pluralistic world call for steadiness, the meeting of challenges head on with deep prayerful embrace and dialogue.

I will use the story of Polynesians and the development of Oceanic culture to point to ways forward. Acknowledging the wisdom of other peoples who have embarked on adventures of faith, I nevertheless offer a contribution from Oceania that has an emphasis on the vital importance of relationships.

I do not relate something of the story of the ancient Polynesians and their courageous voyages in order to perpetuate romantic myths about the people of Oceania that seem to have persisted since the early days of encounter with the West. I am all too aware of political turmoil in Oceania – in recent years in Fiji, Papua New Guinea, the Solomon Islands and in my birth country, the Kingdom of Tonga. There are very real problems to be addressed in the countries of the Pacific Rim as well as elsewhere in our troubled world. But even given the very real problems, or maybe because of them, I am compelled to assert that the response of the ancient people of Oceania to the call of the *moana* is a response and a gift we can share with the world today. We too are called to unprecedented adventures in faith as we move towards the unseen future.

Tangata moana

At a time parallel to that of the biblical Abraham who migrated with his extended family from Ur of the Chaldees to Canaan, the land promised to him by God, the ancient Polynesians also migrated across great tracts of water. About 4,000 years ago, they set out and made their home on the waves in great canoes as they looked for new lands. They brought with them distinctive pottery called Lapita pottery and sometimes these people are called Lapita peoples. They brought livestock – dogs, pigs and chickens. They brought crops – breadfruit, coconuts, sugar cane, medicinal plants, and other food crops including *taro*. These ancestors of the Oceanic world were the greatest of all navigators.

The ancient Polynesians were the first *tangata moana* – Oceanic people. Moving from South-east Asia, as most scholars contend, they swept through the already populated islands of Melanesia and discovered new groups of islands, which are known now as New Caledonia, Vanuatu and Fiji. Around 3,000 years ago, they moved in their canoes further east to Tonga and Samoa. Within the last 2,000 years there have been other movements including sailing north to Hawaii, south-east to Tahiti and the Cook Islands and about 900 years ago south to Aotearoa New Zealand (Thompson and Taylor, 1980, p. 16).

The call to adventure and discovery

The ancient Polynesian people engaged in almost incredible journeys driven by different needs. These may have included the need to look for new reserves of food and the avoidance of conflict. One possibility for migration, put forward by Patrick Kirch, is the social organization of the Lapita people, which meant the first-born sons inherited rights of land and dwelling (see Kirch, 1997, p. 65). Interestingly, as a younger son I can identify with the migration of those younger members of a family – after 4,000 years, this migration of younger Polynesian sons who have limited access to land still happens. Though it cannot be proved, it seems to me that a major motivation of the ancient Polynesians was a deep need to satisfy the spirit of adventure. Without a spirit of adventure, the ancient Polynesians would not have developed fishing craft into great ocean-going canoes. They would not have found the great courage to move onward beyond the horizon – to dare to travel where humans had not travelled before.

The ongoing movement across the ocean is part of the huge heritage of Oceanic people. They are people who were formed and continue to be formed on and by the embrace of the ocean waves. The exposure to the ocean would have contributed to the development of Oceanic culture. To survive, it would have been important that all should have a place and there should be a working together of the members of the canoes or *vaka*, from place to place the word used (with slight variations) throughout Oceania.

Vaka and the spiritual journey

The great ocean-going *vaka* in which the early voyages were made were big enough to carry large numbers of people and supplies. They were carefully constructed in order to withstand giant waves. They were double-hulled voyaging canoes. Large poles were lashed across two canoes and bamboo decking was lashed to the poles, forming a platform on which a hut or huts for storage and shelter were built. The double-hulled canoes provided more stability in the water than a single outrigger. They were fast. 'Polynesian voyaging canoes could slice through the waves at up to 20km an hour, covering 160 km on an average day, much faster than the

European sailing ships still in use just over 200 years ago' (Nicholson, 1999, p. 16).

Later evidence makes it clear that there was a spiritual dimension about the life in the *vaka*. The creator god Tane is invoked in this ancient Tahitian chant for the consecration and launching of a new canoe (Thompson and Taylor, 1980, p. 8):

I sail my canoe
Through the breaking waves,
Let them pass under,
Let my canoe pass over,
O god Tane!

The gods were invoked for protection. Canoes were made with great reverence and were the work of experienced carvers. In the canoes, representations of the gods were often carved. In the building of a Maori canoe, the *tohunga* (the specialist or priest) would select a suitable tree and ask *Tane-Mahuta* (goddess of the forest) for permission to use her child (the tree). The area where the canoe was constructed was regarded as sacred.

Vaka – core of the way of life of the *tangata moana*

The *tangata moana* trace their origins to epic migrations across Oceania. When human migration by land was stopped short by the ocean boundaries, the ancestors of the Oceanic people did not allow the complexity and the mystery of the uncharted ocean to deter them. The challenge of the ocean was accepted.

There is a lack of written resources as to how the deep relational values of the Oceanic people emerged, developed and were sustained. I would argue that the impact of life relationships from within the world of the *vaka* formed the cradle of the emerging culture and world view of the early Oceanic people. After thousands of years, the essence of the early formation of these ancient values remains in the culture of Oceanic people today. Instilled and treasured in the heritage of the *tangata moana* would have been a whole approach to life in constant relationship with fellow seafarers, including women and children, with the environment, the wind, the sky above and the waves beneath and the presence of the gods and goddesses. All those on board would have needed to be in tune together, helping one another in order to arrive safely at their destination. Central to the way of life was communication among those on board the *vaka*, with close participation and engagement. The longer the journey, the deeper would each member come to relate to the others and their bond with the ancestors. The longer the journey, the more deeply aware of the ocean and its life the seafarers would have become, and they also would have been more deeply aware of the shining constellations, which not only guided them but lit their night skies.

As those who have experienced the clear skies of the Pacific will testify, on a clear night they are so alive with stars it seems that you are surrounded and that you might even reach up and touch them. So the ancient Oceanic people lived among the stars and their relationship to them shaped their lives. The heritage of the heavens had been passed down through many generations. Growing up in Tonga, I experienced for myself in formative years time spent in competing with other boys in demonstrating knowledge of the stars, observing their appearance, telling stories about the stars and relating the stars to fishing.

I believe that the core of the Oceanic world view is deeply rooted in the ethos and collective life of the *vaka*. A culture evolved by predominantly land dwelling would have needed to change further as social life was restricted by limited space and bonds were formed to enable epic journeys into the unknown. In this new way of living and the challenge of discovering previously uninhabited islands, common dreams, courage, trust, mutual responsibility, interdependence and hope would be heightened by the voyage. The lives of the ancient Oceanic people were shaped by perseverance, discoveries, excitement, huge hardship and achievement and failure in their endeavours. Life in this new context was very much shaped and nurtured by the Oceanic world. The core of this emerging, transforming belief and culture was their perception of the interconnectedness of the gods, the environment and the life on board the *vaka*. The sense of interconnectedness contributed powerfully to the formation and development of their settlement into their new environment in newly found islands. Life was about relating to fellow voyagers, to the *moana* and to the sky and the gods.

When the ancient *tangata moana* arrived after their long voyages and settled on islands in the Pacific Ocean, it was the way of life of the *vaka*, a world view oceanic in the core of its ethos, that was adapted and developed and continued to be valued and passed on to future generations. Their descendants passed on their identity as people of relational rhythm. Environment, ancestors and human community were integral to the whole of life. People's activities exist in relationship. This was the legacy of the waves of the vast *moana* and its mystery.

The legacy of the waves – dance

> In the beginning God the dancer
> danced the dance of love,
> filling up the emptiness
> of waiting with her rhythm.
> She danced out the universe,

twirled the stars and planets,
held light and dark in either hand
and clapped them into wisdom.

And everything moved
in a circle of love, a circle of love,
And everything moved in a circle of love
and God saw that it was good.
Then God danced the mountains up
and trod the seas deep down.
She creased the land for rivers,
made rivers to hug the land.
Everywhere her footsteps went,
the earth broke into green,
flax and fern and tree and vine,
dancing to the rhythm of love.

Joy Cowley, Creation Dance, a modern psalm,
Psalms Down Under (1996), pp. 22–3

The legacy of the waves is to be found in cultural expression in Oceania today. The singing of hymns often has the deep resonances of the waves breaking on the reef. In the lines of carving, in the weaving, in the making of *tapa* (traditional cloth made from the pounding of mulberry bark), in the design of tattoo, in the songs and in the dancing there are echoes of the movement of the ocean.

Waves danced before humanity came into existence. Waves will continue to dance whether humanity is conscious of the great dance or not. Waves will dance and dance forever. Life in and on the *moana* involves movement. The waves flow. The currents on the surface and deep beneath the surface move. The creatures of the sea – the whale, the shark and even the jellyfish and the plankton – move. The wind moves on the waves. The dance of people takes up the dance of waves expressing strong relationships – the interconnectedness of energies.

Dance is very much a living cultural expression in Oceania. Dance is often deeply expressive. Dance is to be found far away from tourist centres, on outer islands, in remote villages. Dance is an expression of the joy of living. Children learn to dance at a very early age and often seem to have the innate ability to respond to the rhythm of the music and to move with grace. Hands move, eyes move, bodies move, and the songs sung and the flowing movement (particularly of the hands) often tell a story. Dance in Oceania expresses powerfully the synergy of life – the connecting of the heart, mind, and body with creation. It empowers collective functioning and rhythm. In Oceanic dance there is performance in which words are sung but there is also performance in which words do not feature, as in dance to the rhythm of the drums, the stepping of the feet and the clapping of the hands.

The power of the Oceanic dance is felt when people are at one with the whole rhythm of dance. *Mafana* is a Tongan word that is used when you feel rapt or embraced by a situation so that you want to be part of it. This Oceanic expression refers to a warm feeling, a moving from the inner being. *Mafana* happens when the whole performance of the dance embraces the whole gathering. Oceanic dance reaches its highest when all are embraced. Dance has reached a climax when all are brought together and together everyone has something to give and receive.

Tulou, Tulou, Tulou Moe Tolu-Taha Toputapu
Tulou, Tulou
Kau Fakatapu Kihe Vunivalu
Fakatapu Vunivalu
Fa'ahinga Tapu 'Oe Lotu Faka Tohitapu
Fa'ahinga Tapu
Hufanga Atu Talangata 'iate Au
Hufanga Atu 'iate Au

Fai Ki Tu'atatau Koe Pangai – Kafa 'oe Lotu
Ki Tu'atatau

In the presence of the Holy Trinity
in your presence
In the presence of the paramount chief of Fiji
in your presence
In the presence of the Church
in your presence
May we present ourselves
in your presence.

Vaka Lo'amanu, Dance Director/Composer,
English translation: by the author

In August 1997, the Archbishop of Canterbury, George
Carey, with Mrs Eileen Carey, made an official visit to New
Zealand. The Archbishop was not able to include a visit to
Fiji, the headquarters for the Diocese of Polynesia. As leader
of the Diocese of Polynesia in New Zealand, I was responsible for organizing the Diocese's welcome to the Archbishop
at the Mangere Marae Church – Te Karaiti Te Pou Herenga
Waka in Auckland. The community of the Diocese of Polynesia in Aotearoa New Zealand performed a special dance
composed for the historic event.

In the opening verse of the song (quoted above), which
accompanied the dance, the connections are made. The
Triune God is acknowledged first of all, and then the context
is acknowledged – the headquarters of the Diocese of Polynesia is in Suva, Fiji. Although the welcome was in Auckland,
in the tradition, the land where the headquarters is situated is
honoured and takes precedence. And so the leader of Fiji is
acknowledged. Finally, the Church today is mentioned.

The *ma'ulu'ulu* is a type of group dance performed while
people are seated. This dance was chosen to include old and

young, male and female, lay and ordained. The words sung and expressed by the movements spoke of the history of the Church and the purpose and the celebration of the visit. In the *ma'ulu'ulu*, the dancers learned about the story of the Church in a very powerful way. The movement of the bodies was in time with the emphases in the sung story of the major achievements of the Church's mission.

In *ma'ulu'ulu*, there were times for singing, times for action with energetic, robust movements, and times for action and no singing. The bodies moved according to the rhythm of the drum. The whole church, ordained and lay, old and young, danced on the occasion of the visit of the Archbishop. No one was excluded from the dance. They danced as a community. They danced with great joy. They danced to the lyrics, singing with their hearts and moving their hands and bodies in unison with their feet in harmony with the story of God's work in their midst. As I write, I find my hands on the computer also perform in the spirit of the *ma'ulu'ulu*.

The *ma'ulu'ulu* is an example of the many dances in Oceania that are performed in a group. Numbers forming a group may vary from three to a thousand. There are times of moving together, times of movement in different directions, but all the dancers are in time and move to the same rhythm. Sometimes the movement of the dance is serene, gracious and prayerful. At other times the movement is vigorous. All in all, there is togetherness.

Dance of hope

The *ma'ulu'ulu* was taken from its more usual place of performance in Tonga to New Zealand. And its movements caught up people who were Tongan born and Tongans who had been born in New Zealand. It embraced others who were ethnically not Tongan, but from other parts of Oceania.

Of course, it is unlikely that the *ma'ulu'ulu* will become a worldwide dance. But as people of the embracing, moving oceans of the world, if we value relationships and if we rejoice in them, we will attempt to learn to move together in harmony in a metaphorical inclusive dance – the dance that is in rhythm with the heartbeat of the God we have come to know in Jesus.

In the *ma'ulu'ulu* the costumes of the dancers were identical and impressive in their colourful uniformity. But in this world we need to dance together in our differences, finding a way our differences can combine. I first saw the striking collage 'Dance of Hope' on the wall of the artist in Suva. Jane Ricketts is a family friend and she is one of those who are deeply committed to working towards justice and peace in troubled, multicultural Fiji. In the book, *Let Us Celebrate*, she describes the inspiration behind her picture: 'Dance of Hope was inspired by a dance sequence in one of Larry Thomas's plays in which a young Indian girl and a young Fijian boy in traditional dress perform their own cultural dances at the same time but independently. The girl danced to the rhythm of the tabla and the boy to the lali. The dance was a stop/start affair with the boy sometimes threatening the girl with his spear while she shrank away. Gradually however the rhythms of the drums came together and the boy laid down his spear. Then the pair began to dance together still performing their own movements but also, at times, following each other to dance as one. The audience burst into applause. It was a brief but moving interlude. In my picture, I have tried to capture something of the "unity of diversity" of the original performance. Each dancer maintains his/her identity but each is also open to the other to create something new together. Each complements the other' (Ricketts, 2006, p. 71).

'Dance of Hope' calls us to dynamic embracing community in a divided world.

5

The Ocean as Space

God is a refuge and strength,
a very present help in trouble.
Therefore we will not fear,
though the earth should change,
and the mountains shake in the heart of the sea;
though its waters roar and foam,
though the mountain tremble with its tumult.
Be still and know that I am God!

Psalm 46.1–3, 10a

Space

Human beings on earth look up to space – to the heavens –
and wonder at the beauty and the mystery of the stars and
the planets. The ancestors of Oceania were not limited to
looking up at the vast dome of the sky. They also contemplated the ocean and they identified a strong relationship
between the heavenly bodies in the space of the sky and the
waves of the ocean. In the world view of the Oceanic people,
the *moana* and the heavens represented space – space that
allows both being and becoming.

Oceanic people were shaped by the immense and diverse

reality of both the heavens and the ocean. The heavenly bodies of the space above and the *moana* space below and the whole interconnected space were sacred. Within the heritage of the Oceanic people there is a strong respect for the mystery and interconnectedness of life. Life according to forebears is a gift held in a sacred context – a context that gives space that allows for a deep and respectful relationship.

In the Hebrew Scriptures, the psalmist is brought to an understanding of the significance of human beings and their relationship to creation as the heavens are contemplated:

> When I look at your heavens, the work of your fingers,
> the moon and stars that you have established;
> what are human beings that you are mindful of them,
> mortals that you care for them?
> Yet you have made them a little lower than God,
> and crowned them with glory and honour.

Psalm 8.3–4

A deepening awareness of the universe gives understanding not of the insignificance of humanity, but surprisingly gives understanding of the significance of human life to God and, as the psalmist goes on to say, of its significance of human life in relation to creation. In Psalm 46 (quoted at the beginning of the chapter), the psalmist is facing times of change and challenge. The psalmist assures us that God is with us in situations that threaten to overwhelm us. The psalm appeals to us to allow space – stillness.

> Be still and know that I am God.

Psalm 46.10a

To be still is to give space in order to allow for new perceptions and greater wisdom. This chapter puts forward the immense value of providing space, which is not mere physical space, as we approach current crises in this world and in the Church. Space is needed in this world of troubled relationships and diverse thinking. The space required is not meaningless vacuum but deeply respectful space that allows and indeed encourages the presence and contribution of the other, however different.

To allow space is, in the words of Micah the prophet, 'to do justice, and to love kindness, and to walk humbly with your God' (6.8). To allow that sacred space for God and for others, there then is a way forward. There are many calls for conversation or dialogue, for peaceful ways of dealing with diversity and conflict. *Talanoa*, which I am now going to present, is an Oceanic gift and contribution to the whole quest for more listening and dialogue. In the very word itself is the notion of giving grace and space to each other and for one another.

Talanoa is a heritage and part of Oceanic culture today. In the present context of Oceania, besides being used widely in village gatherings, *talanoa* has been developed to address recent religious, economic, socio-political and cultural crises in some parts of Oceania.

We, as people of Oceania, are an integral part of the world. Although we may be perceived as people far distant and isolated in islands scattered in a vast ocean, in this chapter I contend that we speak not as people of the land but people who have been nurtured by the vastness of the ocean and the huge importance in human relationships of life-giving space.

Talanoa – telling stories, giving space

Talanoa comprises two Oceanic words. *Tala* is the word for sharing stories. The nineteenth-century novelist, Robert

Louis Stevenson, went to live in Samoa for the sake of his health. He became known as 'Tusitala', which means 'Teller of Tales'. *Tala* can also mean presenting something deep within oneself or foretelling the future. The story-telling may be about the family, daily activities of life, stories about plantations, weaving, fishing, ancestors, extended family, mystery, humour, fear, gossip, hope, pain, birth and death. Any story has a place because every one belongs and can claim a space. That is where the second part of the word, *noa*, comes in.

Noa is space given by an individual, a group or the environment. It is not mere empty space. In an Oceanic context, when there is a more formal gathering, a particular space is given for story-telling or presentation, even for both. Each situation determines the kind and the nature of space required for the occasion. Associated with any space set aside there is a sense of awe of the presence of those who have gone before, and there is a sense of continuity as the stories related are handed on. In many cases, at the beginning, before the central items that have prompted the gathering, there is a welcoming introduction, which includes the naming of forebears associated with the space in which the gathering is now held. The abuse of the space by foul language or inappropriate stories is frowned on by the listeners, and an indication may be given that abusive and destructive talk should stop. The occupants are protected because there were others before them and they are not alone. There is a collective censorship since sacred space belongs to everyone.

Talanoa is then to tell stories within a community that is open and receptive. *Talanoa* is a common word for sharing conversation and yet within groups it can be a respectful way by which voices are deeply heard. When there are crises and conflicts, when there are differences, the coming together of people for *talanoa* may provide a way forward.

To engage in *talanoa* is to value different stories, different voices, and different contexts as gifts. When people share, they are not isolated. To engage in *talanoa* is to recognize the breadth of community. Above all, *talanoa* honours and celebrates belonging and diversity.

Respect and trust – a modern use of *talanoa* in political crises

My brother Sitiveni Halapua, facilitator, economist, Director of the Pacific Island Development Programme (PDP) in Hawaii, was the first to develop creatively the culture of *talanoa* into a philosophy and praxis for peace and reconciliation in the modern political arena in Oceania. The PDP is a regional body set up to assist political leaders of Oceania in socio-economics and development. The membership of the PDP comprises the Prime Ministers of most of the island states of Oceania. The main emphasis of this programme is research. Academic research has a vital role in enabling Prime Ministers to be equipped for effective leadership. They come together, meeting face to face, strengthened by their own interactions, to share common concerns and discuss research projects. The PDP is not a decision-making body but a consultative body.

The new development of *talanoa*, according to Sitiveni Halapua, was born out of national political and economic chaos in the Cook Islands. In 1996, Halapua was invited by Sir Geoffrey Henry, the Prime Minister of the Cook Islands and Chair of the PDP, to explore an alternative economic model to save the economy of the nation, which was on the verge of bankruptcy. The Asian Development Bank offered a model for economic reform. However, the Prime Minister was not totally convinced of the value of adopting that model, as the nature of the corruption that nearly brought the nation to its knees was both very much related to recent

Cook Islands history and also part of the changing reality of the Cook Islands caused by the various effects of globalization. What was needed was a process for achieving change and economic reform that was appropriate and relevant to the current changing needs.

Halapua searched within the depths of his own soul for models of economic reform. Eventually, *talanoa* emerged strongly in his mind and heart as an ancestral gift that had proved its value in Oceania for thousands of years. In his Web article he explained how his use of *talanoa* came into being: 'I was searching for what can bring [this] diversity together. I thought, let's have a look at our ancestors, because our ancestors must have done something right, otherwise we would not be here today. Then I said it must relate to Talanoa, because when you sit down and share your stories, someone will be talking about yam growing, another person will talk about religion and God . . . But that process allows for diversity, the way we live our lives, our culture. Then I started working on Talanoa to develop it, because you have to articulate it, otherwise non-Pacific Islanders will not understand the philosophy behind Talanoa. So I am writing about it, as well as practising and implementing it – the theory follows the practical application.'

Sitiveni Halapua has argued that *talanoa* has many facets. One is that '*Talanoa* does not have a preconceived agenda. It is very open, you can tell your story' (Halapua, 2007, p. 9). He goes on to say: 'If you give people the opportunity, and they know you respect their voice, they will tell you their stories; that is a universal human phenomenon' (p. 9). Finally, he contended that *talanoa* 'is not a solution, it is not an end result, but it is a process through which you are likely to achieve what is common to people' (p. 10). Ultimately, he said, it 'is based on respect and trust' (p. 10). *Talanoa* is an activity that is oceanic, communal, and oral in nature. It requires face-to-face encounter. People share stories as part of everyday life. Halapua transformed the use of *talanoa* into a tool for modern democracy. This was new.

When Halapua moved *talanoa*, which was already in use in the heart of the community, into the chambers of the Parliaments and both formal and informal circles of political debate, issues of corruption and economic crises began to be dealt with through a *talanoa* methodology. He encouraged and enabled concerned groups – formal and informal, professional, women's groups, non-governmental organizations, church bodies – to talk together and to relate stories and issues that were close to their hearts and had impact on their lives. A vital dimension of *talanoa* for the Oceanic people is this face-to-face interaction. The emphasis on Halapua's use of *talanoa* is on focused and skilful facilitation and on providing a safe forum for listening in which people are able to express concerns without being threatened in any way.

Talanoa has become a contextual vehicle for people to address problems and to make their voices heard in the political arena. This process has helped the people of the Cook Islands and is an extension of a traditional and time-honoured practice that recognizes the place of story-telling/ sharing of concerns in a respectful way. A striking aspect of *talanoa* is that it honours the past, brings the past to the present and enables creative change in moving to the future.

The process of *talanoa* used in the political arena energizes wide, face-to-face participation with people owning and taking responsibility for their own destiny in social and economic development. When the people of the Cook Islands were given the opportunity to talk seriously about corruption, tremendous energy was released from within the community – energy that assisted change. The achievements of the *talanoa* process in economic reform in the Cook Islands paved the way for its further use in other crisis situations in

Oceania. The empowering of people to talk about matters of great importance to their lives has become a process relevant to achieving reconciliation and making peace.

In 1987 Fiji, a nation of indigenous Fijians, Indo-Fijians, Rotumans, other Pacific Islanders and people of European origins, a nation of different religions – Christianity, Hinduism, Islam and Sikhism – suffered two military coups in the same year. My family and I experienced first hand the devastating impact of the coups on ordinary people, as I was then in Church ministry in Suva, Fiji. The churches were divided in their response. Other faiths were confused and traumatized by actions that were carried out supposedly in the name of Christianity. Racial tension increased. People were divided. There was mourning for the land, which had prided itself on the harmony of the races. Fiji was no longer, as a popular adage put it, 'the way the world should be'. Fiji continued to struggle as a nation and hardship increased for the poor of all ethnic groups.

Fiji's political unrest continued and a third coup was staged in May 2000 by a failed businessman, George Speight, and supporters. The then Prime Minister, Mahendra Chaudry, together with members of the Government, were held by an armed squad within the Parliament buildings.

When a new election was held and Laisenia Qarase came into power as Prime Minister, the East West Centre at the University of Hawaii offered help to the Government with a *talanoa* project. Sitiveni Halapua was given the task. He started by drawing together diverse groups including political opponents, religious leaders, former hostages and coup leaders. As the process progressed, both the Prime Minister and Leader of Opposition brought their core groups together for ongoing engagement in dialogue on key fundamental issues that were crippling the nation. The work slowed down when the leader of the Government used delaying tactics as a form of control and domination. A fourth coup took place in

December 2006. This was again an army coup and was led by the Commander of the Army, Frank Bainimarama (see scpi Website, pp. 24–5). However, Halapua stresses that *talanoa* is not itself a solution but is a process towards reconciliation and peace. He has continued with the process in Fiji.

The political upheaval in the Solomon Islands in 2006 was more than the tribal rivalries about which some journalists have generalized. Corruption and hunger for power were central to this crisis. Sitiveni Halapua was invited to the Solomon Islands by the National Council of Peace (NCP). This body was set up by both the Australian and the Solomon Islands Governments as a concrete attempt to find a way forward towards reconciliation. The work of the NCP was funded by the United States of America. Halapua, with the assistance of the Chair of the NCP, was the first to visit the Weather Coast, the headquarters of Harold Keke, the leader of an uprising. Halapua spent weeks walking from village to village meeting, talking, persuading and negotiating opportunities for the *talanoa* process. When the time came that people themselves felt safe and ready for this act of trust, leaders of the different tribes brought their people with them. This was the first such meeting that brought together the diverse peoples of this area. Deep appreciation of reviving their heritage was evident. People took ownership of the process. It was during this meeting that people themselves shared their stories of how seven Melanesian Brothers were brutally killed (as related later in this chapter) and also how a Roman Catholic priest was shot. People felt safe enough to share the story, and this was a process that could lead towards reconciliation.

While further processes of the *talanoa* path for political reconciliation were being planned for the Solomon Islands, a political crisis in the Kingdom of Tonga erupted. Halapua was invited by the Government of Tonga to negotiate with the leaders of the Government and the Pro-Democracy

Movement in order to try to avert the possibility of bloodshed, which was lurking on the horizon. The agreed process for further talks towards more democratic representation in Tonga was not honoured by the Prime Minister of Tonga. This resulted in rioting and the burning of the centre of the capital, Nuku'alofa.

While Halapua was still engaged with the crisis situation in Tonga, a Solomon Islands senior civil servant told him that people on the Weather Coast had taken up the process of the *talanoa* and transformed it in their indigenous way. When *talanoa* is presented in terms of contextual values, people identify with it and understand that the process is something of their own heritage. Credit needs to be given to the Melanesians themselves for the way *talanoa* has been developed within the Solomon Islands.

Melanesian *talanoa*

In 2003, seven Melanesian Brothers were brutally murdered by followers of Harold Keke on the Weather Coast of Guadalcanal in the middle of the political crisis in the Solomon Islands. This tragedy sent shock waves through people in Oceania and beyond. For those who know anything of the wonderful work of the indigenous Anglican religious order of the Melanesian Brotherhood, it seemed an almost unbelievable tragedy. The humility and faithful service of the Brothers are well known.

The Melanesian Brotherhood was founded in 1925 by Ini Kopuria, a Solomon Islander, who was born on the island of Gaudalcanal in 1900. Ini Kopuria became a member of the native police force. During a time of recovery after a knee injury, he received a life-changing vision of Christ. This led to his commitment to evangelistic activity among his own people and the early formation of this unique indigenous

religious order in which Brothers take temporary vows that
are renewed.

Kopuria was a man of reverence for God, a man of prayer.
The Brothers were prayerful from the start. They were courageous, setting out two by two, unarmed, with no possessions
or food. They stayed in villages, which were often hostile,
where they aimed to live the life of the people in the place.
They talked and shared and worked together with people
before moving on. They penetrated into remote areas. They
carried the gospel of Jesus Christ. This pattern set for the
Order by Kopuria has remained, though numbers have
swelled from the humble beginnings of the six brothers who
originally joined Kopuria. There are now Melanesian
Brothers in the Solomon Islands, Vanuatu, Fiji, Papua New
Guinea, the Philippines, Canada and England.

When the Diocese of Polynesia explored indigenous
approaches to make our mission more relevant in our multi-
racial and pluralistic context, the simple and dedicated
approach of the Melanesian Brothers stood out. As a theological student in the 1960s I was sent to work alongside the
pioneering Melanesian Brothers in an Indo-Fijian sugar-cane
farming community in the middle of the interior of Ba, on
the western side of Fiji. I experienced how dedicated the
Melanesian Brothers were. In 2002 I conducted a survey on
the role of the Church in a political crisis situation in the
Solomon Islands. In that survey, I consulted widely with
many church leaders, including members of the Melanesian
Brotherhood. When I was in the Solomon Islands, I was
made aware of the high regard in which the Melanesian
Brothers were held. People honoured the way they went
about serving and working for reconciliation and peace
among their own people in many parts of the Solomon
Islands. They won the trust of most people in urban as well
as rural areas. They stood out as friends. They were neutral
and had access to people at many levels. They were messen-

gers of hope. Not with theological jargon but with simplicity and story-telling, their lives and words spoke of Christ – the Prince of Peace.

The way of life of the Melanesian Brothers expresses the heart of *talanoa*. It is face-to-face encounter with people in order to listen to their anguish and concerns, in order to hear their fear and their dreams but also to tell stories of faith and love. This is the gift of the Order passed on by Brother Ini Kopuria. This commitment to peacemaking discipleship in word and lifestyle has been costly for the Order and the death of the Brothers witnesses to that. Richard Carter, who at the time of the deaths of the Brothers in 2003 was serving as Tutor and Chaplain to the Order, writes in the wake of their deaths: 'One thing I am certain: these seven men will live on in the hearts and minds of our Community. Their sacrifice seems too great and hard to believe. The Community sat up through the night telling the stories of these Brothers and trying to come to terms with the enormity of their loss. And yet beneath the trauma there is peace too – the knowledge that each of these young men believed in peace and goodness. They knew there was a better way. They were prepared to oppose violence and risk much. At the end of the day they stand out against all acts of brutality which are at present disfiguring our world, and bravely, boldly, and with love, lived out what most of us proclaim only from the safety of the church. Oh how much the worldwide Anglican Church at the moment should learn from their witness! And when such real-life issues are so much at stake in our world, is this not what the gospel should be?' (Carter, 2006, p. 159). For the Melanesian Brothers, humble discipleship, which includes the *talanoa* of the gospel of Jesus, is a gift to be shared. I believe also that they have a strong message for the wider Church.

Four gifts of *talanoa* for the wider world

Space

Talanoa gifts space for a process of coming together to emerge. It provides a safe atmosphere for interaction. Space provided is not for some to seize or dominate, rather the space is a creative space set aside to enable the welfare of all. In picture language of the five oceans of the *moana*, each ocean flows and shares its own distinct gifts and differences and there is room for all. The impact of the interaction and interconnectedness flows out from their togetherness. Together five oceans provide a powerful contribution that gifts the planet earth with life in a way that none of them can do without the others. To engage in *talanoa* is to celebrate that which is in common and it also means the gaining of understanding of the contexts of differences. *Talanoa* honours the numinous and that which cannot as yet be understood, and it gives room for interaction.

Justice

Talanoa offers a way of securing justice. In order to realize justice, the safety of the space is imperative. Individual or collective stories all belong and should have rightful space within the gathering. Within this context, no one story has more space and value than any others. Every story, long or short, individual or collective, important for some and perhaps irrelevant for others, should be accepted. No storyteller should leave feeling excluded or unheard. Diversity enriches. What is good for others is also a blessing for all.

Listening

Talanoa is about the sacredness of listening. In order for all to hear one another, talking must go hand in hand with listening. *Talanoa* includes listening to others, to the environment and to God. Pick up a cowry shell, place it against your ear and listen shhh . . . shhh to the sound of the 'ocean'. The sound of the waves heard as from within the shell is not the music of actual waves breaking on a beach but the sound of the water in your inner ear. This illustrates how when we listen we may truly hear more than we realize – we may hear that which is deep within us.

Talanoa is about sensitive and intentional listening. When people are prepared to listen to complete stories and those stories are not in isolation from those who have gone before and from the voices of the environment around, then something of the sacredness of listening is experienced.

In listening there is room for silence – the profound contribution of silence, beauty and serenity. Powerful interaction happens at a time of silence. When the ocean is silent, this does not mean there are no dynamic activities taking place. The reciprocity of the *talanoa* embraces vocal and silent interactions, respects and gives space for them all.

Listening is a vital dimension of *talanoa*. Listening and story-telling are vital parts of the continuing human journey. The ability to listen is an art. In order to be able to function together in the *vaka* (the canoe) on the voyage, the honouring of the space of each was vital. Some were responsible for the reading of the signs from the stars or the position of the moon and the direction of the sun. Others observed the movement of the waves and the currents. The wind and behaviour of birds were among the many voices that needed to be heard clearly. Different voices contributed to the overall survival and to arriving at the destination of the voyage. The *vaka* would not arrive there if some of the voices

were heard seriously while others were suppressed or under-
mined.

Dialogue

Talanoa is sacred space for dialogue in which all are valued
and have profound contributions to offer. There is hospitality given – hospitality that is at the very root of the formation of community. Engagement and participation are not
coerced but rather offered as a privilege – as an opportunity
for learning and insights, for the forging of human relationships, for the bearing of one another's burdens in times of
hardship or loss. No one is called to suffer or celebrate alone.
Space given is sacred for those who listen and also for the
story teller. Exchanged stories are life – they convey life.
'Dialogue is a process through which we uncover and reveal
our human grandeur. Dialogue withers when our hearts are
closed to the infinite possibilities of the other and we assume
we already know all we need to know about them. Dialogue
flourishes when it is conducted in an open-minded spirit of
discovery based on compassion, on the desire to build on
what we have in common and transform our differences into
resources of value' (*SGI Quarterly*, 2007, p. 28).

Let us spread out the mat so that we can start the process of the conversation

An important dimension of the art of listening in Oceania is
expressed in the custom of the sitting arrangement. There is
a Tongan proverb: *Fofola e fala ka tau talanga*. The literal
translation is: 'Let us spread out the mat so that we can start
the process of the conversation.' Most Oceanic people sit on
the floor or on the grass when they make space for story-
telling or meeting. When a mat is put on the grass or floor of

the veranda or sitting-room, it signals a warm sense of welcome to friends or guests. The custom of the laying out of a mat in the presence of guests and friends is not only a sign of welcome but also a time-honoured invitation for conversation, telling stories and dialogue.

Let us spread out the mat of welcome. Let us give one another the space of hospitality. Let godly converse begin. In his book *Where God Happens: Discovering Christ in One Another*, Rowan Williams quotes the Desert Fathers and Mothers, among them Anthony the Great: 'Our life and death is with our neighbour. If we win our brother, we win God. If we cause our brother to stumble, we have sinned against Christ' (Williams, 2005, p. 13).

The God who calls us to stillness – gives space so that we may truly know and experience something of the immense and embracing love – is the God who 'makes wars to cease to the end of the earth' (Psalm 46.9).

6

Waves of Justice and Peace

But let justice roll down like waters,
and righteousness like an ever-flowing stream.

Amos 5.24

Peace . . . Peace . . . Peace . . .
Deep peace of the running wave to you
Deep peace of the flowing air to you
Deep peace of the quiet earth to you
Deep peace of the shining stars to you
Deep peace of the Son of peace to you.

The Iona Community (Adam, 1985, p. 91)

The patron saint of Oceania – Peter Chanel

Peter Chanel was proclaimed patron saint of Oceania by the Roman Catholic Church in 1954. He was born after the French revolution in Bresse in the French countryside. Peter's association with the local parish at an early age led to his being chosen by the parish priest to be one of the few boys undertaking Latin classes at the presbytery. His education was further encouraged by succeeding priests and on Passion Sunday in 1817, the day of his first Communion, he made up his mind to become a missionary. In 1819 Peter Chanel entered a seminary. After eight years in different seminaries, he was ordained priest in 1827.

In 1837 Bishop Pompallier sent Peter Chanel as a missionary to Futuna in the Pacific Ocean. In Futuna, Chanel encountered tribal rivalry and warring. He suffered wavering support and then the displeasure of the emerging 'king' of the area, Niuliki. In 1839 Niuliki mounted a major battle against the people of a rival district in Futuna. He was badly defeated. This defeat meant loss of face and his *mana* (charisma/ prestige) was diminished. A scapegoat had to be found. Niuliki attributed his defeat to the presence of the new mission. In such a testing context, Chanel and the few he gathered around him struggled with limited stocks of food further reduced by a hurricane.

The increasingly hostile situation did not deter Chanel's focus on engaging in mission. He faithfully persevered. 'The future saint went on patiently with his work. He taught the need to forgive enemies, tended the sick and wounded, and seemed to be unaware of Niuliki's cooling regard' (Garrett, 1982, p. 98). Chanel's health was failing rapidly but his ministry continued until, on 28 April 1841, he was brutally murdered by Musumusu, Niuliki's son-in-law. Garrett writes: 'As he bled, some of his converts heard him say that all was well and death was his gain' (p. 98). The story of Peter Chanel is one of faithful and courageous commitment to his call and to the mission of the Church.

There are many others, including people indigenous to Oceania, who have served with humility and courage. The lives of many Oceanic people and their work in the spread of the gospel are not recorded in detail, if at all. But Chanel's humble and sacrificial ministry and mission have contributed to life-giving waves of the good news of Jesus Christ within Oceania.

The gift of a pectoral cross

> I ask not only on behalf of these, but also on behalf of
> those who will believe in me through their word, that they
> may all be one. As you, Father, are in me and I am in you,
> may they also be in us, so that the world may believe that
> you have sent me. The glory that you have given me I have
> given them, so that they may be one, as we are one, I in
> them and you in me, that they may become completely
> one, so that the world may know that you have sent me
> and have loved them even as you have loved me.

John 17.20–23

Given the significance of this story within the Roman
Catholic Church, it seems unlikely that an Anglican should
inherit the pectoral cross of this first canonized saint in
Oceania. But, strangely and wonderfully, a pectoral cross of
Peter Chanel was given to my father when he was consecrated the Suffragan Bishop of Tonga and Assistant Bishop
to the Diocesan Bishop of Polynesia in August 1967. On the
historic occasion of Fine Halapua's consecration, among
those who were present was a good friend and ecumenical
colleague, Bishop John H. Rogers, the Bishop of the Roman
Catholic Church in Tonga. He presented Bishop Fine
Halapua with a gift from Rome, a pectoral cross owned by St
Peter Chanel. According to Bishop Rogers, the cross had
been set aside by the Roman Catholic Church to be given to
the first Polynesian in the Pacific to be consecrated bishop. A
cross of St Peter Chanel was presented generously in 1967,
not to a Roman Catholic, but to an Anglican. This is the
pectoral cross I wore at my own ordination as the Bishop for
the Diocese of Polynesia in Aotearoa New Zealand and Co-
Presiding Bishop.

Relationships between the Roman Catholic Church and

the much smaller Anglican Church are strong in the Kingdom of Tonga. The pectoral cross from St Peter Chanel given
to my father speaks of an attempt to forge relationships and
to live out ecumenism in Oceania. I share the story of the
cross of St Peter Chanel to illustrate how generosity can be so
much alive at the heart of the Church.

There is a tantalizing mystery in the giving of the pectoral
cross that still intrigues our family. Some of our forebears on
my father's side come from the Futuna and Wallis Islands.
Where were our forebears at the time of the martyrdom of
Peter Chanel? However, the story demonstrates how, in the
love of Christ, relationships reach across boundaries and
divisions. I realize this story will have counterparts in other
parts of the world. I tell this story because it is close to my
heart. As I honour the humility of the saint who originally
wore the cross, I honour the faithfulness and humility of
those who gave the cross to my father.

Waves of justice and peace

The gift of the cross of St Peter Chanel is, among other stories
of reaching out with warmth and generosity across divisions
in the Church, an answer to the prayer recorded in John 17,
which flowed from the heart of Jesus Christ. At the heart of
the Christian faith is the reconciling love of God. The cross
on which Jesus died is the great focus of unity. Empowered
by the reconciling love of God experienced in Jesus, energized by the life-giving Spirit, we must reach out to one
another across our differences.

In our unity, in our embracing of one another even in our
diversity and disagreement, we must discover anew our
mission to a threatened and divided world – we will together
set up waves of creativity and life that will reach to the ends
of the earth. We are called to engage in mission together. As

waves are interconnected with one another and to the *moana* (oceans), so we are called in relationship with one another to proclaim in word and action God's reign of justice and peace.

The account that follows is a story of how churches in Oceania are together finding a voice to challenge the abuse of the *moana*. It is about a new momentum and a deepening awareness of our common heritage and responsibility as human beings. It is about an urgent call to address life-threatening issues. This call is not just to the Church in Oceania but to the wider Church and to all people concerned with life on planet earth.

A prophet bishop and churches of Oceania and climate change

The story of the pectoral cross of St Peter Chanel is an expression of ecumenical relationships within the churches of Oceania. The Pacific Conference of Churches (PCC) to date is ecumenical and Oceanic and includes the Roman Catholic Church as a full member. Other churches, besides the Anglican Church, are Methodist, Reformed, Congregational, Lutheran and Protestant. The PCC comprises major Christian churches from most island states in Oceania, from the Marquesas and French Polynesia in the east to New Caledonia and Papua New Guinea in the west, from the Cook Islands and Tonga in the south to the Islands of Micronesia in the north.

Since 1961, the Churches in Oceania, under the umbrella of the PCC, have been working together on common issues to carry out the mission in our context and in our world. The PCC is unique in the World Council of Churches in that it is the only WCC region in the world that includes the Roman Catholic Church as a member. Through the Pacific Catholic

Bishops' Conference, the Roman Catholic Church became a full member of the PCC in 1976.

In the 1980s in Oceania, the Roman Catholic Bishop, Patelisio Finau SM, emerged with a prophetic voice on issues to do with justice and peace. Bishop Finau became a charismatic President and leader of the PCC. He strongly addressed the issues of nuclear tests in French Polynesia, militarism in Bougainville, Papua New Guinea, Fiji, Solomon Islands and East Timor, the dumping of nuclear waste in Oceania and the political and social plight of people in his homeland, Tonga. During his presidency of the PCC, his leadership on the care for the integrity of creation impacted on the Church and also in regional politics. Kevin Barr in his tribute to the leadership of Bishop Finau writes, 'Many were happy to call Bishop Patelisio a prophetic priest, others, who opposed him, called him a political activist' (*Pacific Journal of Theology*, 1994, pp. 35–7). Like St Peter Chanel, Bishop Finau with his vision and commitment to mission did not allow political intimidation or hostility or hardship to deter him from his call. In 1993, he made this statement in an interview on Radio Australia: 'I believe we are stewards of God, accountable to God. Creation is God's gift to humanity and we are to use it properly. Not to master it in the sense of wasting it. We are to take care, tender loving care, and to make sure that it is beneficial to all people – to all humanity – and more and more we realise we cannot be so domineering and think that our species is the only one that matters. Many other varieties of life are in God's design and are there for God's glorification. Yes, they are there for our use – sensible use – and also for our joy. At the same time we are responsible and accountable to God in the way we use God's gifts to us' (*Pacific Journal of Theology*, p. 99).

Bishop Finau died suddenly on 3 October 1993. His visionary work continues. Finau's prophetic voice and advocacy for the integrity of creation have not been blown away by the varying winds and hurricanes of the region. In September 2007 the 9th Assembly of the PCC met in American Samoa. This Conference comprises representatives from 35 member churches, associates and observers from different parts of Oceania and the world. Issues impacting on Oceania addressed during in the last 30 years have included nuclear testing, the dumping of nuclear waste in the Pacific Ocean, the invasion of multinational corporations, globalization, militarism and HIV/AIDS. At the meeting in American Samoa delegates became acutely aware that the impact of climate change is at the present time one of the greatest threats to the lives of many in Oceania. With the help of modern technology and Powerpoint presentations, the plight of fellow Pacific Islanders was vividly set out. First-hand stories – stories of waves of destruction caused by climate change – were told. People from Tuvalu and Kiribati in Micronesia shared their stories. This was timely face-to-face *talanoa*. As we have already seen, the daily reality of many Oceanic nations is being affected by the rapid loss of low-lying coastal lands, the increased severity of hurricanes and tropical storms, and the threats to drinking water and the land used for planting of food crops as sea water seeps into land because of rising sea levels. Corals, which are integral to many of the Oceanic island states and home for many marine species, are bleached and destroyed. The stories moved the delegates of the churches to their inner core. How can we hear the stories of multitudes of marine species? Who can tell their stories? Members of the Conference were reminded of the violence in recent years of nuclear tests in French Polynesia and in some parts of Micronesia. But as horrendous as the consequences of nuclear testing to Pacific people and the environment were, the threat to survival from climate change is unparalleled and ongoing. Through the vivid, graphic presentations and the first-hand stories there was a deepening realization within the Conference that, because of climate change, powerless people were being violently abused in the environment of their own island homes.

The response of the churches gathered in American Samoa to the stories of our own people concerning the impact of the climate change was a deep, informed and passionate debate. There was a resulting statement. I was there as a delegate and a prime mover of the resolution that has now become the 'Statement from the PCC 9th General Assembly on Climate Change' (see the Appendix, p. 96 below). The Statement from the PCC expressed the heart and mind of the whole Conference. Taking seriously the expressed realities of people in Oceania, the Statement was also informed by stories and insights from the wider bodies of the World Council of Churches and the United Nations. Some key paragraphs are quoted below:

> We deplore the action of industrialised countries that pollute and desecrate our Oceania, our Moana. Our Moana, our [O]ceania is our gift from God and as a part of God's creation, it is our duty as dwellers of this ocean to be stewards of this gift. It is our theology and our covenant with God and with one another. We invite the worldwide community to work with us. We are a part of the whole body of Christ. When our low-lying atolls of Oceania are affected by the effects of climate change, we all suffer as a result . . .

> We the members of the Pacific Conference of Churches [believe that we are] called by God to:

> ➤ Affirm our commitment to care for the Oceania as our response to God's love for creation.
> ➤ Declare the urgency of the threat of human induced effects of climate change to lives, livelihoods, societies, cultures and eco-systems of Pacific Islands.

➤ Dedicate ourselves to engaging our churches in education and action on climate change.
➤ Commit ourselves to ecumenical collaboration among our churches and with other religious and secular bodies in the Pacific and beyond that [to] increase the effectiveness of our national and regional efforts.

The Churches in Oceania have made a collective stand in order to honour the ocean entrusted by God and to give voice to their grave concerns. The Churches have spoken and continue to speak against human-induced climate change that does violence to creation and threatens the very existence of life in some parts of Oceania.

Before missionaries arrived over 200 years ago, Polynesians as Oceanic people celebrated a holistic heritage. Crawford writes: 'For the Polynesians, gods and spirits were their ancestors. They had no concept of distinct natural and supernatural worlds. Their gods had created the universe and everything in it, and therefore people and nature were related as one. The land and the sea, the sun and the sky, the plants and the animals were all part of that heritage to which they and their ancestors belonged' (Crawford, 1993, p. 41). The *moana*, the home and the abundant source of life, the pathway of our ancestors and our heritage – a heritage to be shared with planet earth – is threatened. As present-day *tangata moana* – people of the ocean – we would argue that the gift of creation in Oceania is also a gift to the planet. In Oceania we are called to be faithful custodians of the gift of our environment, but because our lives on planet earth are interconnected, there is a great need for other parts of the world to acknowledge that what happens to islands in the Pacific Ocean has far-reaching significance. The voices of the powerless people of Oceania are ignored to the peril of planet earth. In the words of a press release from the United Nations Development Programme: 'Pacific people face the greatest risk of becoming poorer, getting displaced from their homes and regressing in their development as a result of climate change. While the Small Islands Developing States in the Pacific are amongst the lowest carbon emitters, they will be the first to suffer from climate change. In the next ten years if the average temperature were to increase beyond two degrees Celsius, sea level rises will see a number of Pacific islands disappear from the face of the map, the United Nations Development Programme's Human Development Report 2007/2008 warns' (19 December 2007).

Instead of turning to the gods and spirits the churches of Oceania relate to the Triune God – God the Creator, Jesus the Redeemer and the Life-giving Spirit – who in interconnected relationship provides the Source of Love and Life within which the whole creation finds its true purpose. In Jesus Christ we encounter the human face of a God of interconnected relationship. Through the good news of Jesus Christ, the ancient world view of the Oceanic people is transformed. The *tangata moana* are enabled to speak of the *moana* in terms of the gift of a loving God and the interconnectedness of all life in the planet earth. The gift of creation is a concrete expression of our Creator's love and embrace. The Pacific Ocean or any of the oceans are not commodities to be abused by the violence of human exploitation. The tragic consequences of climate change are manifestations of the way human greed and weakness are instrumental in the abuse of the life of the *moana*.

In a recent book on the ethics of global warming, entitled *A Moral Climate*, Michael Northcott writes: 'Acting rightly with respect to the earth is a source of hope, for those who so act give expression to the Christian belief that it is God's intention to redeem the earth, and her creatures, from sinful subjection to the oppressive domination of prideful wealth and imperial power. Such actions witness to the truth that the history of global warning has gradually unfolded; that those poor or voiceless human and non human beings whose prospects climate change is threatening are neighbours through the climate system to the powerful and wealthy. And Christ's command in these circumstances is as relevant as ever: "love your neighbour as yourself"' (p. 285). Many contemporary scholars and scientists agree that climate change is the impact of unbridled human activities. Together with our sisters and brothers in the wider Church and with people who care, there is a need to work urgently towards the addressing of problems caused by climate change and to halt the possibility of future devastation.

This is a paragraph from the Statement from the PCC General Assembly on Climate Change (see Appendix) which calls for togetherness in our prophetic mission:

We call on our sisters and brothers in Christ throughout the world to act in solidarity with us to reduce the causes of human-induced climate change. We issue this call particularly to churches in the highly industrialised nations whose societies are historically responsible for the majority of polluting emissions. We further urge these countries to take responsibility for the ecological damage that they have caused by paying for the costs of adaptation to anticipated impacts.

7

Deep Ocean

If my lips could sing as many songs
as there are waves in the sea:
if my tongue could sing as many hymns
as there are ocean billows:
if my mouth filled the whole firmament with praise:
if my face shone like the sun and moon together:
if my hands were to hover in the sky like powerful eagles
and my feet ran across mountains as swiftly as the deer;
all that would not be enough to pay you fitting tribute,
O Lord my God.

Jewish Prayer, *Hear our Prayer: An Anthology of Classic Prayers*,
2005, p. 25

The call of the conch

A large shell, a conch, has been used and is still used in different parts of Oceania as a musical instrument, a signalling device and a means of communication. A hole is made in the shell at the conical end so that lips may surround the hole. The hole allows air blown through the lips to reverberate within the shell. The blowing of the conch requires acquired skill, but the result is a haunting sound that seems to come from the depths of the ocean. In Oceania the shell trumpets have called people together for religious rites and funeral occasions. The blowing of the conch has heralded success in fishing and in tribal wars. In New Caledonia, the Kanak have used conch-blowing at the beginning and ending of a harvest. The use of the conch at times of renewal of life such as for births and harvests leads Raymond Ammann to suggest that there is strong connection between the blowing of the conch and the very essence of life. He goes further: 'It seems that in taking into account the varied characteristics of the conch, its origin in water, the spiral form of its tube, its use as a container of magic herbs and its possibilities as a musical instrument, the Kanaks have obtained from it a metaphor for their conception of life' (Ammann, 1997, p. 36).

Throughout Oceania today, although the *lali* (wooden drum) has often superseded the use of the conch in many settlements and villages, the conch is still used to call people on special occasions. It heralds that which is deeply significant. It may herald good news or impending danger. The blowing of the conch sounds a welcome. It may call people together for meeting or celebration. And the conch is used like the ancient Jewish ram's horn, the shofar, to call people to worship God. As a means by which people are called to worship, the sound of the conch is a voice from the Pacific Ocean. The sound of the conch represents the voice of the *moana* calling people together. Its penetrating, resonating voice seeks in-depth response from all who hear. The *moana* calls us to adventures that are beyond paddling in the shallows of the immensity of God's love. The *moana* calls us to embrace and embark on the waves of that love.

This book is my way of 'blowing the conch' to call people to experience and share together in the wonders of God's love. An image from Oceania is used here, as other images are used throughout the book, to help further our creative listening and response to the call of God in our challenging times.

Deep experience

My last experience of a tropical hurricane was at the time
when I was Dean of the Cathedral of Suva, Fiji. It was at the
beginning of a new year, on a Saturday evening, that the
winds began to rise and the radio broadcasts began to inform
us of an impending hurricane. We had spent the day happily
preparing for the seventieth birthday of a good friend. He
was an Australian who had adopted Fiji as his home. He was
well known in Suva and had many friends but he regarded us
as his family, having no family of his own in Fiji. His friends
included Muslims and Hindus and so we prepared traditional Polynesian food – fish and chickens and root crops –
excluding both pork and beef. We anticipated a wonderful
birthday party and indeed the guests arrived happily and part
of the food was consumed, but both we as hosts and the
guests became aware of the winds swirling round the house,
and soon it became evident that the party should end early so
that hurricane shutters could be erected and preparations
could be made to secure the safety of people and property.
The guests needed to return to their families before branches
and broken electrical wires began to fly round and make
travel difficult.

That night the hurricane hit in full force. Early on Sunday
morning, knowing that there would perhaps be no services
because of the severity of the hurricane and the devastation
in Suva, I nevertheless travelled the deserted road a short
distance to the cathedral to assess the damage. On the large
veranda surrounding the cathedral I found people sheltering
– there were the homeless poor and a few people from outside Suva who had been stranded. I quickly returned home
and we loaded the car with the feast from the previous
evening – a large quantity of food – which the guests had left,
and my wife and I returned to the cathedral and opened the
doors wide. There were leaks in the roof, broken windows

and pools of water on the floor. The driest part of the cathedral was where the altar stood and where the sacraments were shared Sunday by Sunday and throughout the week except Saturday. We moved to the driest part of the cathedral and invited those who had been sheltering from the storm to join us. On the altar we laid the feast and we shared the food with those who needed warmth, safety, breakfast and loving companionship. It was one of the most moving and memorable Sunday mornings in my life and ministry. We were caught up in meeting human need at a deep level, in a radical hospitality that was about sharing what we had with one another. The post-hurricane experience of simple sharing was a pointer to what Eucharist is about – a participation in large, overflowing and inclusive generosity.

The risen Christ on the shores of Galilee

After the immense devastation of the suffering and death of Jesus, the friends of Jesus encountered the dawn of a new day (John 21.1–7). The risen Christ on the shores of Galilee came to his friends in their reality – he came to their fishing ground, their empty nets and their meal on the beach, he came to their grief and their guilt and their confusion. The risen Christ came when all appeared lost. In the encounter with the risen Jesus on the shores of Galilee there was a transforming experience of the depths of love. In the story of Peter's encounter with the risen Christ, we hear of words of deep love – deep love that is to be shared.

The deep

In the Oceanic world when we talk about the *moana* – the ocean – what often comes to mind is that which is deep. A sense of life that is rich, full of meaning and yet, at the same time, surrounded by mystery is all described by the use of the word *moana*. Oratory and many hymns and poems that speak of deep experience in human life often include *moana* as metaphor. When the word *moana* is closely linked with words such as love, mystery, commitment, space, passion, then the meaning of the words is intensified.

The Oceanic world is not alone in using the ocean as a metaphor for that which is vast and which is deep. In Psalm 139 the psalmist speaks of the breadth and depth of God's presence and care and that presence and care extend beyond the limits of the sea.

> Where shall I go from your spirit? O where shall I flee from your presence? If I ascend to heaven, you are there; if I make my bed in Sheol, you are there.
> If I take the wings of the morning and settle in the farthest limits of the sea,
> Even there your hand shall lead me, and your right hand shall hold me fast.

> Psalm 139.7–10

The ocean has been used as poetic picture language for God – the ocean as mysterious and living, as vast and deep, as conceiving and carrying, as embracing and giving life – and so it has come to express something of eternity. An example of the use of the depths of the sea to describe something of the wonder of God is found in a seventeenth-century hymn. Referring to God, a verse of the hymn reads:

> How great a being, Lord, is Thine,
> Which doth all beings keep!
> Thy knowledge is the only line
> To sound so vast a deep.
> Thou art a sea without a shore,

A sun without a sphere;
Thy time is now and evermore,
Thy place is everywhere.

John Mason c. 1645–94

Samuel Trevor Francis, whose life spanned the nineteenth and the twentieth centuries, wrote of the deep love of Jesus as a deep ocean:

O the deep, deep love of Jesus!
Vast, unmeasured, boundless, free;
rolling as a mighty ocean
in its fullness over me.
Underneath me, all around me,
is the current of Thy love;
leading onward, leading homeward,
to my glorious rest above.

Samuel Trevor Francis 1834–1925

Hymns in Oceania have used the ocean as a metaphor for God's deep love. The *Ocean Carol* was written for children of different ethnic groups in Fiji and has been both sung and danced in Suva and beyond:

Mary smiles and rocks her baby to sleep.
God's love is deeper than our ocean deep.
Jesus is born for us, we've heard,
we'll pass it on and spread the word:
God's love is deeper than our ocean deep.

Wise men nod and shepherd leave their sheep:
God's love is deeper than our ocean deep.
so let us kneel and worship him,

just where we are – is Bethlehem:
God's love is deeper than our ocean deep.

Children laugh and waves for gladness leap:
God's love is deeper than our ocean deep.
The sunshine of our hearts is here,
to chase away our dark and fear:
God's love is deeper than our ocean deep.

Islands sing! Wake up from drowsy sleep!
God's love is deeper than our ocean deep.
The Manger, Cross and Cave declare,
that all may now God's glory share:
God's love is deeper than our ocean deep.

Susan M. Halapua, Suva, 1980

The God who put the rainbow in the heavens has also put rainbow colours within the ocean. Hidden inside myriad shells are the luminous colours of mother of pearl. The iridescence in the shells, on an infinitesimally smaller scale, reflects something of the potential of the ocean as metaphor to describe the immensity and intensity of the shining light of God. In this chapter, I use the *moana* – the ocean – as a metaphor for God, a metaphor that speaks with enormously deep resonances.

Discovering our identity

Within the flow of the chapters of this book, there is sociological and theological analysis of an Oceanic world view. There are reflections on the formation of the identity of the Oceanic people through their encounters with the realities of the ocean. From the time voyaging ancestors set out in their twin-hulled canoes across vast tracts of water, this identity has emerged within the depth of our people as we have engaged with one another and with our environment.

There is a great need for us as human beings integral with the life of planet earth to know who were are in order to relate to one another and to creation. We need to relate to one another, far more than superficially, across ethnic, religious and ecological divides. We need to understand the perspectives of male and female and relate to each other with our differing sexual orientations, gay or heterosexual or transsexual. We need to relate to one another across divisions of language and culture, of affluence and poverty, of power and powerlessness. We need to be instrumental in healing our world of humanity and our differing but interconnected environments.

The Anglican Communion is experiencing crisis. At the time of writing, it seems very evident that the worldwide Anglican Communion is struggling with an identity crisis. Do the four 'Instruments of Unity', the Archbishop of Canterbury, the Primates, the Lambeth Conference and the Anglican Consultative Council, represent the essence of the Anglican identity? To what extent does our common Anglican legacy of Scripture, tradition and reason embrace holistically our diverse reality today? Was the concept of reason a contribution of the Enlightenment period? What would be the new theological relationality that would express an Anglican Communion of the twenty-first century, when most Anglicans are from outside Europe and North America? How does the identity or lack of identity of the Anglican Communion further or hinder the mission of the Triune God? The Virginia Report says this: 'Every act of God is an act of the undivided Holy Trinity. The very being of the Church is thus dependent upon the outpouring of God's gracious love, the love of Father, Son and Holy Spirit. The experience of the truth of the revelation of God in Jesus Christ came to the disciples as a gracious gift. What the disciples experienced at

Pentecost in Jesus Christ was that communion of life with God which was present at creation and which will be perfected in the fullness of time' (pp. 9–10). The Anglican Communion is God's gift. The need to celebrate that core of our God-given faith, which has held us together for many generations, remains.

Since the Gospel accounts of alarmed disciples on the threatening waves of the Sea of Galilee and their waking of the one who calms the sea and who calms their hearts, the boat has been used to represent the Christian community. Deep questions arising from our Oceanic context are: how are we recognizing the risen Christ in the midst of our Anglican Communion and how are we listening together to his voice so that our *vaka-moana* (outrigger) may move forward in mission?

As we are aware of Christ's presence and together listen to his voice rising above our consternation in the Anglican Communion, the crisis that is threatening the mission of the Church may be grasped as an opportunity. We may begin to listen more deeply to the needs and pain articulated within the Communion, to the needs and pain of our sisters and brothers, to the needs and pain of our fellow human beings.

The many Provinces and nations represented in the Anglican Communion all have – like Oceania – their own particular heritage. Environment and history have shaped structures and cultures, spiritualities and ways of expressing the gospel of Jesus Christ. There is a great need to celebrate the richness of our diversity as we engage in mission together. When we discover more fully who we are in Christ, we discover more fully our true identity and our potential to reach out together and embrace others. This is the wonder of the gospel of Jesus Christ.

Identity from the perspective of Paul

The Apostle Paul sets out our identity as Christians. He writes with passionate clarity about new identity in Christ. He speaks from his own encounter with the risen Christ who transformed his own life on the road to Damascus.

> For all who are led by the Spirit of God are children of God. For you did not receive a spirit of slavery to fall back into fear, but you have received a spirit of adoption. When we cry, 'Abba! Father!' it is that very Spirit bearing witness with our spirit that we are children of God, and if children, then heirs, heirs of God and joint heirs with Christ – if, in fact, we suffer with him so that we may also be glorified with him. (Romans 8.14–17)

In this passage Paul, writing to the church in Rome, is helping believers to understand the privilege of their new identity. The letter to the Romans describes the profound relationship with God that is gifted through Christ by the power of the Spirit. As members of an emerging community in Christ, as members of the body of Christ, believers 'led by the Spirit of God are children of God' and as beloved children and 'heirs of God and joint heirs with Christ', they have access to an intimate relationship with an infinitely loving God, 'Abba! Father!' There is access to an intimate relationship with God, not just in the present. Believers, as children of God, have immense hope for the future. Through suffering there is a glorious hope.

The profoundness of new identity in Christ is to Paul what God's grace is all about. The new identity in Christ relates to all creation:

> For the creation waits with eager longing for the revealing of the children of God; for all creation was subjected to

futility, not of its own will but by the will of the one who subjected it, in hope that creation itself will be set free from its bondage to decay and will obtain the freedom of the glory of the children of God. We know that the whole creation has been groaning in labour pains until now. Romans 8.19–22

I am inspired, encouraged and energized by Paul's ownership and celebration of his identity in Christ. In Paul's understanding, Christ is God's free gift of God's love not only for humanity but for all creation. In Christ lies Paul's power for life and the source of his distinct contribution to mission.

Paul's new identity in Christ, his life-transforming experience, helped him reach across divisions of ethnicity and belief. Jew as he was, shaped by an orthodox tradition of Judaism, he found in Jesus Christ the forgiving, embracing love of God. This love of God could reach out to him in the depth of his need and not only to him, but to others very different in religious and cultural background – the Gentiles. Paul, with his pedigree within Judaism, may well have been regarded as the most unlikely candidate for the mission to the Gentiles, but now Paul is regarded as the great Apostle to the Gentiles. He was able to reach out farther than he could in his previous wildest imaginings. For the first Christian communities, he was the great boundary breaker.

At the end of the same chapter of his letter to the Romans, Paul sets out his conviction about the depth of God's love in Jesus Christ:

I am convinced that neither death, nor life, nor angels, nor rulers, nor things present, nor things to come, nor powers, nor height, nor depth, nor anything in all creation, will be able to separate us from the love of God in Christ Jesus our Lord. (8.38–9)

Within the ocean of the love of God we will find new life with one another and new life to share with the peoples of planet earth and with creation.

Theomoana – moving beyond boundaries

Where the road runs out and the sign posts end,
where we come to the edge of the day,
be the God of Abraham for us;
send us out upon our way.

Lord you were at our beginning,
the faith that gave us birth.
We look to you our ending,
our hope for heaven and earth.

When the coast is left and we journey on
to the rim of the sky and the sea,
be the sailor's friend, be the dolphin Christ;
lead us on to eternity.

When the clouds are low and the wind is strong,
when tomorrow's storm draws near,
be the spirit bird hovering overhead
who will take away our fear.

Colin Gibson, 'Where the Road Runs Out', 1991

When the first Polynesians' land journeys were cut short by what is now known as the Pacific Ocean, they observed, calculated, invoked their gods and together, aided by insights gained from their experience of the interconnectedness of the ocean waves, the winds and the heavenly bodies, they designed and constructed the first *vaka moana*. The courage of these first Polynesians can encourage us as we navigate the new waters of the future. When we reach the apparent end of what we have known, there is the need to launch out into the deep, and dare to travel beyond the horizon.

Theomoana is presented as a new gift from the Oceanic world experience, to contribute a particular perspective that may assist our new journeys together in mission. The word *theomoana* has been constructed in order to help me express deep realities emerging from experiences in this part of the planet. It is acknowledged here that experiences and emerging realities may resonate with those of others in different parts of the world. There are deep realities, which may often be understood by people with very different backgrounds. There are mysterious links and affinities between people, which cannot easily be defined in spoken or written words.

Theomoana brings together two ancient words from two different contexts. *Theo* is the first part of the word 'theology', 'the science of God or of religious truth', which is derived from the two ancient Greek words, *theos* (God) and *logos* (word, or reasoned discourse), and may also be defined as 'speaking about God' (see Rayment-Pickard, 2007, pp. 74 and 138–51). *Moana*, the second part of *theomoana*, is, as we have discovered, an ancient Polynesian word for the ocean.

Theomoana is an approach, a conversation or dialogue with theology. As each person in the Oceanic group dance has a part to play within the dance, so each section of the Church has a movement of grace to offer in the worship and mission of God. I am aware that throughout the ages there have been many contributions to doing theology and there are many contemporary contributions, but this 'movement of grace' from Oceania is offered alongside the work of other thinkers and scholars from different parts of the Church and world. *Theomoana* is an oceanic perspective of the embraced love of the Trinity.

The inclusive love of the Triune God is the subject of

theology. Theology gives expression to the identity of the Church and its mission. The God who came to share our humanity in Christ has long been controversial. The human face of God's embrace of love and justice became a threat to belief in the gods of Rome, including the Emperors. God's love became incarnate in Christ and the power of the cross did not sit well with the Greek ideology of a god in isolation from the rest of the world. However, the violence of persecution of the early Church in the first three centuries did not deter giants of faith from faithfulness to the truth of God's love revealed in Christ by the power of the Spirit.

The life, death and resurrection of Jesus Christ shaped New Testament theology (see Hooker, 2007, p. 75). Controversy about the nature of God and the relation of Jesus Christ and the Holy Spirit resulted in the first great ecumenical council in Nicea in the year 325, under the leadership of Athanasius, and the Church began to formalize the doctrine of the Trinity. What we now know as the Nicene Creed affirmed the belief that Jesus Christ is 'of one being with the Father' and that the Holy Spirit 'proceeds from the Father and the Son' (*A New Zealand Prayer Book*). The Three Persons, the Father, Son and the Holy Spirit, are eternally interconnected in the whole being and redemptive work of the one God (Olson and Hall, 2002, pp. 15–50).

In the word *theomoana* – 'God the Ocean' – *moana* is used to express the world-encompassing, interconnecting nature of God. The use of '*moana*' points to the God of flowing unity, whose being is ever life-giving, dynamic and embracing. The use of '*moana*' provides a way of expressing the power of God's loving embrace which Christians have experienced throughout the ages. The use of '*moana*' is gender-free and inclusive and with *theo* is a new way of expressing the dynamic being and nature of God whom we experience as the Creator God, Jesus Christ the Son and the life-giving Spirit.

Theomoana attempts to unveil the essence of the love of the Triune God with emphasis on the depths of that embrace not as theory but rather as encounter with embracing love. *Theomoana* is a call to move courageously beyond boundaries that restrict the mission of the Church. In order to meet the challenges of this century there is a need to go back to origins in the early Church, to learn from the Church's development over the years and to construct the appropriate *vaka* to take the mission of the Church forward.

Why *theomoana*? *Theomoana* is put forward as a way of offering gifts to theological thinking. In the prayerful construction of the word, I would challenge theologies that are not grounded in the experience of human beings within creation. There is a need within the Church for emphasis on the relational experience of the faithful presence of God – the loving God who relates to us intimately and relates also to creation. There is a need to acknowledge that the power of God's presence draws us to respond by our moving in mission together.

As the waves of the oceans of this world break over reefs and embrace the coastlines, so the waves of the God whom we may describe and celebrate as the great *moana* embrace us without ceasing. *Theomoana* underlines that our thinking and relating to God are also about our thinking and relating to one another. The depth and width of the *moana* embrace all of creation.

Why *theomoana*? In the five oceans of the world – the Pacific, Atlantic, Indian, Arctic and Antarctic – there is immense diversity. Though the oceans with their diverse life may literally be poles apart, even in their differences they may be a source of life for all the planet earth. Each ocean finds its completion in the others. *Theomoana* emphasizes that we are part of one another. This concept of *theomoana* can be seen in terms of the body of Christ. *Theomoana* intentionally departs from a dualistic approach to theology which is trapped in Gnosticism and Platonic philosophical under-pinnings. Such an unjust legacy undermines the glory of God in creation and in culture. The crisis in the Anglican Com-munion is compounded by a changing of a diverse Anglican Communion into North (Europe and North America) and South (Africa, Asia, South America and Oceania). The God of the oceans hold us in our diversities and our diversities truly may be life for one another.

Why *theomoana*? The oceans of the world have long called seafarers to venture beyond the horizons – to make new journeys of exploration. So thinking and relating to our great God calls us to make new ventures in faith, breaking through what we may have presumed were limitations. Like Paul, we are called to be boundary breakers in our time, meeting challenges head-on as *vaka* confront ocean waves and finding new creative ways forward in mission. We are called to forge relationships with those we never dreamt would be friends, discovering that they are made in the image of a gracious loving Creator.

Why *theomoana*? The *moana*, meaning ocean, existed before human life came into being. The word *moana* is very deeply rooted in creation and speaks of the immense work of creation. The very construction of the word *theomoana* speaks of God's care of the whole of creation. It is a theo-logical and ecological approach that challenges the human, arrogant tendency to treat the planet earth and its life with disrespect. *Theomana* advocates a humility that honours the creation as God's gift. This is of vital importance at this time when abuse of the gifts of planet earth has been so great that there is now threatening global disaster in the form of climate change.

Why *theomoana*? Our oceans are mysterious and inter-connected and their immense mystery and interconnected-ness reveal just something of the greatness of our God. The concept of the Triune God provides an expression of God in relationship with the planet earth, including humanity. The invitation to the Anglican Communion by the Archbishop of Canterbury to consider a model of covenant, to assist in its returning to the very *manava* (source of life) of the Communion's existence in the mission of God, is an invitation to explore an authentic model of life giving in our relationships with God and with one another. Crises potentially tearing apart the church are not in isolation from division and conflict in the wider world. *Theomoana* presents a gift of *talanoa* (godly conversation and profound listening) as a way forward in enabling people to connect – to enter communion. It is in Christ that *talanoa* is located and energized.

From the oceans we are freely gifted oxygen, climate, food and interconnectedness. Most of the living species find a home within waters of the ocean. *Theomoana* speaks of many and diverse gifts in creation. As one ocean flows into another, so *theomoana* speaks of God's love, which flows freely and unconditionally, gifting life without ceasing. *Theomoana* puts forward a way of life that is a response to immense and unconditional gifting. *Theomoana* celebrates that in Jesus Christ we encounter the one who lived out among us, the gracious, unconditional gifting of God who invites us to be part of that free flowing life which is the life of eternity.

The waves of the oceans dance. *Theomoana* celebrates that there can be a joyous dancing together even in our diversity. The dance to which the Triune God calls us is a celebration of loving communion. We are all called to dance the Dance of Love. All are welcome to participate.

Appendix

 PACIFIC CONFERENCE OF CHURCHES

Statement from the 9th Assembly of the Pacific Conference of Churches on Climate Change

We, the members of the Pacific Conference of Churches, meeting at Kanana Fou Theological College in American Samoa from the 3rd–9th of September 2007, are acutely aware of the effects of climate change on our Moana, our Oceania.

We deplore the actions of industrialised countries that pollute and desecrate our Oceania, our Moana. Our Moana, our Oceania is our gift from God and as a part of God's creation it is our duty as dwellers of this ocean to be stewards of this gift. It is our theology and our covenant with God and with one another. We invite the worldwide community to work with us. We are a part of the whole body of Christ. When our low-lying atolls of Oceania are affected by the effects of climate change, we all suffer as a result.

We stand at the Turanga Wae Wae (place of ownership/ guardians of the gift) of the Pacific Ocean and as guardians of this Ocean, it is our duty to protect and safeguard this gift for our future generation.

We, the members of the Pacific Conference of Churches believed called by God to:

➢ Affirm our commitment to care for the Oceania as our response to God's love for creation.
➢ Declare the urgency of the threat of human induced effects of climate change to the lives, livelihoods, societies, cultures and eco-systems of the Pacific Islands.
➢ Dedicate ourselves to engaging our churches in education and action on climate change.
➢ Commit ourselves to ecumenical collaboration among our churches and with other religious and secular bodies in the Pacific and beyond that will increase the effectiveness of our national and regional efforts.

We call on our sisters and brothers in Christ throughout the world to act in solidarity with us to reduce the causes of human-induced climate change. We issue this call particularly to churches in the highly industrialized nations whose societies are historically responsible for the majority of polluting emissions. We further urge these countries to take responsibility for the ecological damage that they have caused by paying for the costs of adaptation to the anticipated impacts.

We call on our global ecumenical movement to pressure all countries to ratify and implement the Kyoto Protocol especially highly industrialized nations such as the United States of America and Australia which to date have not ratified the Protocol.

As Pacific Churches we encourage companies that are major producers or consumers of fossil fuels to support a transition toward less carbon-intensive economies, reduced energy usage and the development of cleaner, renewable energy sources.

We invite church-related specialized ministries for emergency response, development and advocacy to integrate climate change and adaptation projects into their policy-development, education and advocacy.

As a people we express appreciation to the World Council of Churches for its support of the Pacific churches on the issue of climate change. We call for the inclusion of the climate change programme as a high priority of the programme of the WCC. We will take responsibility to keep the churches informed on current developments.

We, member churches and national councils of churches of the Pacific Conference of Churches, commit the appropriate resources towards the following specific actions on climate change:

1. In solidarity with the people of Kiribati, Tuvalu and the Marshall Islands we call upon the churches of the Pacific to be welcoming and compassionate churches to our brothers and sisters from the above countries who wish to resettle in our respective Pacific countries.
2. Advocacy for a regional immigration policy giving citizens of countries most affected by climate change, especially sea-level rise, rights to resettlement in other Pacific Island nations or Pacific regional countries of their choice.
3. Advocacy for a mitigation policy binding the Pacific Forum Island countries to reduce emission rates of carbon dioxide by 30% of 1990 levels by 2020 and by 60%–90% by 2050, (consistent with the need identified by the Inter-Governmental Panel on Climate Change, IPCC, to keep temperature increases to less than 2 degrees centigrade) by investing in renewable forms of energy and energy conservation and efficiency.
4. Advocacy for an adaptive policy binding the Pacific Forum Island countries to develop and implement appropriate strategies to adapt to climate change where possible without deterioration in quality of life, social cohesion and Pacific island cultures.

5. Advocacy for an inter-regional sea level rise financial assistance scheme to finance the cost of mitigation, adaptation and resettlement.

6. Undertake an initiative to look at the roles and responsibilities of the sending and receiving churches to help prepare intending immigrants, to welcome and help resettle them into their new homelands.

7. Work to address wider issues relating to unsustainable development, many of which are made worse by or contribute to the increasingly negative impacts of climate change.

8. Urge delegates to the PCC General Assembly to organize a public prayer and 'Walk Against Warming' in Pacific Island Countries prior to the meeting of the Conference of the Parties (COP), Thirteenth session and Conference of the Parties serving as the meeting of the Parties to the Kyoto Protocol (COP/MOP), Third session, in Bali, Indonesia, Dec 3–14 2007.

9. Facilitate the formation of a network or coalition of agencies advocating adaptive and mitigative action to prevent and address catastrophic climate change in the Pacific and providing relevant scientific information for the lay population.

References and Further Reading

Adam, David (1985), *The Edge of Glory: Prayers in the Celtic tradition*, London: SPCK.

Ammann, Raymond (1997), *Kanak Dance and Music*, New York: Kegan Paul International Ltd.

Bevans, Stephen B. (1992), *Models of Contextual Theology*, Maryknoll, New York: Orbis Books.

Byatt, A., Fothergill, A. and Holmes, M. (2001), *The Blue Planet: A Natural History of the Oceans*, London: BBC Worldwide Ltd.

Carter, Richard A. (2006), *In Search of the Lost: The Death and Life of Seven Peacemakers of the Melanesian Brotherhood*, London: Canterbury Press.

Chester, Tim (2005), *Delighting in the Trinity*, Grand Rapids: Monarch Books.

Cousteau, F. (Introduced) (2006), *Ocean. The World's Last Wilderness Revealed*, London: Dorling Kindersley Ltd.

Cowley, J. (1997), *Psalms Down-Under*, Wellington: Catholic Supplies (NZ) Ltd.

Crawford, Peter (1993), *Nomads of the Wind*, London: BBC Books.

Garrett, John (1982), *To Live among the Stars: Christian Origins in Oceania*, Geneva and Suva: World Council of Churches.

Gibson, C. (1991), *New Journeys Songbook*, Melbourne: Joint Board of Christian Education.

Gunton, Colin (1991), *The Promise of Trinitarian Theology*, New York: T&T Clark Ltd.

Halapua, Sitiveni, (2007), 'Talanoa – talking from the heart', in *SGI Quarterly*, No. 47.

Halapua, W. (2003), 'The Vanua', in *Tradition, Lotu and Militarism in Fiji*, Lautoka: Fiji Institute of Applied Studies.

Hau'ofa, E. (1993), 'Our Sea of Islands', Waddel, E., Naidu, V. and Hau'ofa, E. (eds), *A New Oceania: Rediscovering Our Sea of*

Islands, Suva: University of the South Pacific in association with Beake House.

Hoiore, Celine (2003), 'Some Polynesian perspectives on birth' in *Proceedings of Theology in Oceania Conference, Dunedin 1996*, Pearson, C. (ed.), Dunedin: Centre for Contextual Theology.

Holden, Sara (2007), *Planet Ocean*, Oxford: New Internationalist Publications Ltd.

Hooker, Morna (2006), 'The nature of New Testament theology' in *The Nature of New Testament Theology*, Rowland, C. and Tuckett, C. (eds), Malden, MA: Blackwell Publishing.

Howe, K. R. (ed.) (2006), *Vaka moana; Voyages of the Ancestors. The Discovery and Settlement of the Pacific*, Auckland: David Bateman Ltd.

Hutchinson, S. and Hawkins, L. (2004), *Oceans: a visual guide*, NSW: Weldon Own Pty.

Kemp, Janine (2007), 'Jesus' Galilee' in *A Journal of Theology and Ministry*, No. 32, reo 9.

Kirch, P. V. (1997), *The Lapita Peoples: Ancestors of the Oceanic World*, Malden, MA: Blackwell Publishing.

Koser, Khalid. (2007), *International Migration: A Very Short Introduction*, Oxford: Oxford University Press.

Lal, Brij V. and Fortune, Kate (2000), *The Pacific Islands: An Encyclopedia*, Honolulu: University of Hawai'i Press.

Nicholson, John (1999), *Fishing for Islands*, NSW, Australia: Allen & Unwin.

Northcott, Michael S. (2007), *A Moral Climate: The Ethics of Global Warming*, Maryknoll, New York: Orbis Books.

Olson, Roger E. and Hall, Christopher (2002), *The Trinity*, Grand Rapids, Michigan/Cambridge, UK: William B. Eerdmans Publishing Company.

Pfitzner, Victor and Regan, Hilary (1998), *The Task of Theology Today*, Edinburgh: T&T Clark Ltd.

Hugh Rayment-Pickard (2007), *50 Key Concepts in Theology*, London: Darton Longman & Todd.

Ricketts, Jane (2006), *Let Us Celebrate*, ECREA and CCF Project.

Schreiter, R. J. (2003), Forward to revised and expanded edition, in *Models of Contextual Theology* by Stephen Bevans (1992), Maryknoll, New York: Orbis Books.

Stenson, Marcia (2007), *Illustrated History of Antarctica*, Auckland: Random House.

Thompson, J. and Taylor, A. (1980), *Polynesian Canoes and*

Navigation, Institute for Polynesian Studies, Brigham Young University, Hawaii.

Trewby, Mary (ed.) (2002), *Antarctica*, Toronto: Firefly Books Ltd.

Twist, C. (consultant) (2005), *1000 Facts on Oceans*, Great Bardfield: Bardfield Press.

Williams, R. (2005), *Where God Happens: Discovering Christ in One Another*, Boston: New Seeds.

Hear our Prayer: An Anthology of Classic Prayers (2005), Oxford: Lion Hudson.

A New Zealand Prayer Book He Karakia Mihinare O Aotearoa (1989), Auckland and London: William Collins Publishers.

Your Will be Done: Reflective Writings, Prayers and Hymns (1984), CCA Youth.

Journals/Reports/Websites

In *SGI Quarterly. The possibilities of dialogue* (2007), No. 47.

The Pacific Journal of Theology, Series 11, No. 11, 1994.

Waves, Tides and Shallow-Water Processes (1989), prepared by an Open University course team, Oxford: Butterworth-Heinemann.

Bainimarama, Frank, Web: http://www.scpi.nz/docs/Pacific Ways of Talk.pdf

Dahl, Terje, *Goodbye Tuvalu*, Web: http://www.sydhav.no/terje/tuvalu-e.htm

Halapua, Sitiveni, Web: http://unpan1.un.org/intradoc/groups/public/documents/UN/UNPAN022610.pdf

The Virginia Report (1999), Lambeth 1998 report by The Anglican Communion, Harrisburg, PA: Morehouse Publishing.

Acknowledgments of Copyright Sources

The author and publisher are grateful for permission to include copyright extracts from published sources. Every effort has been made to trace copyright ownership, and apologies are made to those who have not been traced at the time of going to press. Information will be gratefully received on any omissions or inaccuracies in this respect.

David Adams, 1995, 'Peace . . . Peace . . . Peace', The Iona Community, in *The Edge of Glory: Prayers in the Celtic Tradition*, SPCK.

George Appleton, 1985, 'A New Hebridean Prayer', in *Oxford Book of Prayer*, Oxford University Press.

'Jewish Prayer', 2005, in *Hear our Prayer: An Anthology of Classic Prayer*, Lion Hudson.

Bernard Narakobi, 1984, 'A Psalm from the Pacific', in *Your Will be Done: Reflective Writings, Prayers and Hymns*, CCA Youth.

Acknowledgments

This book has been made possible because of the contributions of so many people – so many I cannot name them all. But here I thank unnamed people, past and present, who have played a part in bringing to birth the manuscript.

My deep gratitude to Christine Smith and her able team from the SCM and Canterbury Press. Christine responded with grace when we began the process of talking about the possibility of putting my ideas into writing and exploring the possibility of publication. For her foresight and encouragement, together with the professionalism of her team, I am most grateful.

I have turned to colleagues and friends for their comments on the script and am grateful for suggestions, insights and encouragement. I am grateful to Professor Kanayathu Koshy from the University of the South Pacific, Suva, Fiji, the Rev. Dr. Allan Davidson from St John's Theological College and the University of Auckland and the Rt. Rev. John Bluck from the Diocese of Waiapu. I am grateful to Lois Anderson, my very able executive assistant, who typed and set the script and indebted to Hilary Monteith who patiently and meticulously proofread the text and made wise comments.

I give thanks for my family for their support. Sue, my wife has been my constant companion, ever alongside the journey of the book. Without her understanding and courage, my vision, passion and commitment would not have found expression within these pages.